Making Japanese-Style Lamps & Lanterns

By Edward R. Turner

Hartley
& Marks
PUBLISHERS

For Bud Wood,
my long-time friend and mentor.

Published by
HARTLEY & MARKS PUBLISHERS INC.
P.O. Box 147 3661 West Broadway
Point Roberts, WA Vancouver, BC
98281 V6R 2B8

Text & Illustrations © 2002 by Hartley & Marks Publishers Inc.
Book design by John McKercher
Composition by The Typeworks
Photographs by Ken Mayer
Printed in China

LIBRARY OF CONGRESS CATALOGING-IN-PUBLICATION DATA
Turner, Edward R., 1940–
    Making Japanese-style lamps & lanterns/ by Edward R. Turner.
        p. cm.
    Includes index.
    ISBN 0-88179-198-9
        1. Lamps—Japan. 2. Lanterns—Japan. 3. Woodwork. 4. Decoration and
ornament—Japan. I. Title.

TT197.5.L34 T87 2002
648'.08—dc21   2002025005

CONTENTS

Introduction 5

Projects

Appendix

Introduction

*Gleam of blossoms in the treetops
On a moonlit night.*
—BASHO

The refinement and beauty of handmade Japanese woodwork are unique to Japan's culture, geography, and history. These lamp and lantern designs for bedside, floor, overhead, freestanding, and outdoors, will give woodworkers an appreciation for the deceptive simplicity of traditional Japanese design, and result in objects that are beautiful and useful.

Japanese interior design reflects the knowledge that the shapes and structures that we live with should be influenced by nature. Japanese wooden lamps or *andon* are made with the understanding that the light in our homes should suggest the bright clean light of the morning sun and the soft, searching light of the moon reflecting off the trees. A warm glow emerging from behind thin and delicately textured paper stretched on a light hardwood frame is attractive and distinctly Japanese.

The Japanese woodworking ethic places primary emphasis on the importance of the material. Wood ought to be shaped, writes Dr. Sherman Lee, by the "carefully reticent hand of the artist." Japanese woodwork reflects the mores of a country whose arts and crafts have evolved in a small area, pressed in by hills and surrounded by water. Japanese design emphasizes the natural qualities of local materials such as bamboo, fiber paper, stone, maple, and cedar. One can also see traditional Japanese design concepts such as simplicity, asymmetry, and the careful use of negative space at work in these lamps: The shapes are spare and simple; heavy wooden lids and solid legs suggest the natural shape of a tree. The shades themselves demonstrate the careful use of white space. The impression left by these lamps and by traditional Japanese design in general, is one of clarity and elegance, at once simple and profoundly complex.

Japanese lamps and lanterns look handsome in any room. Subtle lighting, thoughtfully placed, can lend a sense of intimacy, stillness, and peace to the plainest interior. These lamp and lantern designs are adaptable to many circumstances and work in harmonious combination to create an inviting atmosphere. And for those who would like to expand their explorations into Japanese woodwork, the lamps perfectly complement other elements of a traditional Japanese room or *nihon-ma*. You may want to try your hand at the heavy (*fusuma*) or light (*shoji*) sliding doors covered with cloth or paper, or position your lamp to illuminate a *tokonoma* alcove or corner where you display your most special objects.

In choosing projects for this book I included only designs that could be made without specialized tools or techniques. The most sophisticated equipment needed is a small tablesaw or bandsaw. The majority of the work can be done using standard, inexpensive hand tools. The materials, including the electrical fittings, should be readily available.

I encourage anyone to attempt a challenging project they might otherwise shy away from if the only hurdle is the lack of a piece of equipment needed for a short time, such as a jigsaw or bandsaw. Try the generosity of a neighbor or friend and then complete the rest of the project using standard woodworking tools.

The materials recommended for each project are suggestions only. There is no reason, for instance, that softwood cannot be substituted for hardwood. I encourage you to contribute to the uniqueness of the project by substituting materials where appropriate.

A Note About Electricity

Because each lamp described here works with a 120-volt electrical current, which can be potentially lethal, you must adhere to strict constraints when wiring up the lamps. The two wires must never come into contact with one another when the lamp is plugged into an electrical socket. If you alter any of the designs or construction methods in this book, make sure that nothing causes the insulating covering to be worn away. The electrical light socket and wires must be firmly attached to the lamp at all times, the wires must be connected to the socket, and the switch and plug must be installed only as directed by the manufacturer's instructions for each. All the wiring and socket attachment tasks must be completed before the lamp is plugged in.

Mini-fluorescent bulbs are an excellent choice for these lamps. Their output is greater than an incandescent bulb of equivalent wattage and they are very much cooler. However, all light bulbs give off heat and paper can be ignited even by a low-wattage bulb. No material should be closer than $1^1/_2$" from any bulb. For more information on bulbs see the Appendix on page 122.

Throughout this book I refer to lamps as "light fixtures," meaning any construction designed to hold a light bulb in place. An electrical fitting refers to a light socket only, with or without a switch and a nipple (mounting device). Some of the following projects are referred to as "lamps." To me a lamp is a light fixture in which the light source is partially shaded to reduce glare and to direct the light emanating from the bulb. The light source in a "lantern" is completed or partially enclosed with one or more translucent lenses.

Cherry Blossom (Sakura) Table Lantern

This 15" tall lantern is ideal for setting the mood of a room. A pair of them is even better. The construction technique is relatively simple given the great charm of the finished product. Any hardwood such as cherry, maple, or walnut is suitable for making the lantern and a 15-watt mini-fluorescent screw-in light bulb will provide a safe and pleasant glow.

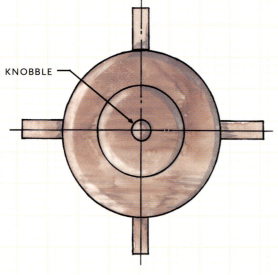

KNOBBLE

Top View

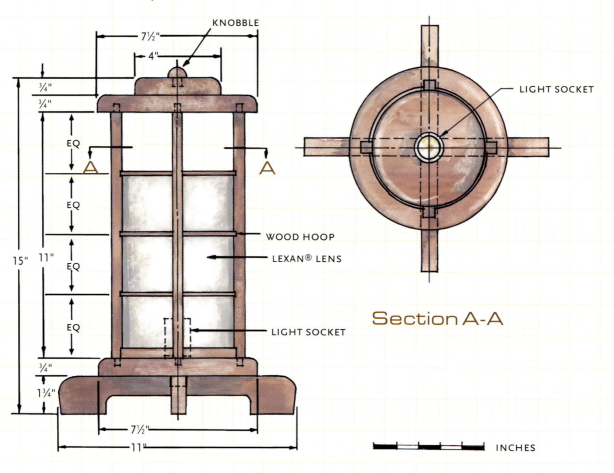

7½"

4"

KNOBBLE

¾"

¾"

EQ

A   A

EQ

15"   11"

EQ

WOOD HOOP

LEXAN® LENS

EQ

LIGHT SOCKET

¾"

1¾"

7½"

11"

Side View

LIGHT SOCKET

Section A-A

INCHES

Method

1. Using ³/₄" stock, cut one disc 4" in diameter and round the upper edge of the perimeter with sandpaper.

2. Again using ³/₄" stock, cut two discs 7¹/₂" in diameter. Round the upper edge of the perimeter of each. These will be the top and bottom of the lamp. Drill four holes, ¹/₄" in diameter by ³/₈" deep, in the upper surface of one and the underside of the other. These holes are centered on a 2⁷/₈" radius from the center of each disc and equally opposed to each other (Figure 1).

3. Cut four squared (¹/₂" × ¹/₂") pieces, 11³/₄" long from ¹/₂" stock and shape the ends of each into

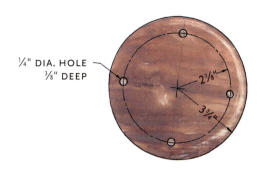

¹/₄" DIA. HOLE
³/₈" DEEP

2⁷/₈"

3³/₄"

Figure 1

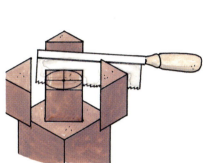
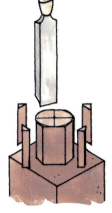
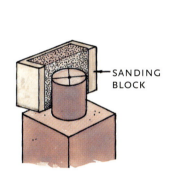

SANDING BLOCK

Figure 2a

Tools

- Bandsaw or jigsaw and a small crosscut handsaw
- Drill (hand or electric) with ¹/₄" and ³/₈" diameter drill bits
- Chisel – ¹/₂" wide
- Utility knife
- Clothes iron
- Screwdriver
- Drafting compass

Materials

- Hardwood (cherry, maple, walnut, etc.)
- Disks – three cut from one-by-eight wood, 24" long, two: 7¹/₂" diameter and one: 4" diameter
- Uprights – four, each ¹/₂" square by 11³/₄" long
- Feet – two, 1" × 1³/₄" × 11" long
- Hardwood edge banding – three ¹/₄" wide strips and one ³/₈" wide strip each 45" long

(this is available at most home improvement stores)
- Thin Lexan® sheet – 8¹/₂" × 17³/₈" (this is available at plastic supply stores)
- Standard electric light socket and nipple with four feet of electrical wire with a switch and plug attached
- Carpenter's glue – white or yellow

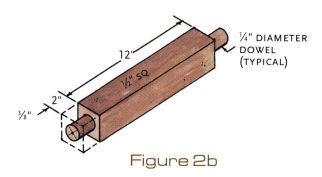

Figure 2b

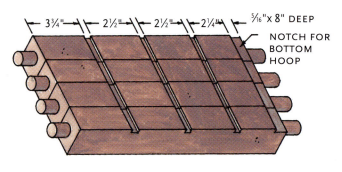

Figure 3

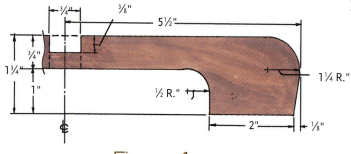

Figure 4
(half-pattern for 11" long "foot")

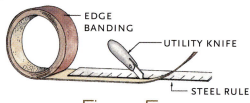

Figure 5

$1/4$" diameter dowels, $3/8$" long, as shown in Figures 2a and 2b.

4. Cut four notches $1/8$" deep in each of the squared pieces, by lining them up side by side and marking off the distances as shown in Figure 3. Hold or clamp the four pieces together and saw them out at the same time to ensure they line up exactly. Use a sharp chisel to "clean up" the bottom of each notch.

5. Cut out two "feet" from the $3/4$" stock using the half-pattern shown in Figure 4. Cut a $3/4$" to $3/8$" deep notch in the center of the top of the foot (Figure 4) and cut the same notch on the underside of the other foot in order to form a perfect lap joint.

6. Now we can turn to the most interesting feature of this project: the four hoops. These hoops are made from natural wood edge banding used in plywood furniture construction. Edge banding is available at most lumberyards in a variety of hardwoods. It comes in coils, usually $3/4$" wide and twenty-five feet long. The wood has a heat-sensitive adhesive backing that can be activated by a hot iron or heat gun. To make the four hoops (one $5/16$" wide and three $3/16$" wide), the edge banding must be "stripped" as shown in Figure 5. Each hoop will require at least

45" of banding. Once this is done, cut a $5^{1}/4$" diameter form from scrap wood that is at least $^{1}/2$" thick. Line up the material for each hoop on one edge of this form to ensure that it will coil straight and flat. Stick one end down with heat to hold it in place; this can later be released with a thin, sharp knife (see Figure 6).

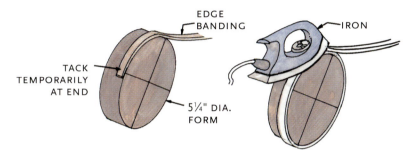

Figure 6

7. Wrap each hoop around the form six times to build up to a thickness of approximately $^{1}/8$". Line up the ends of the hoop material with each other as shown in Figure 7, and taper them with sandpaper. The edges of each hoop can be finished flat and smooth by moving the hoop back and forth and in a circular motion over an upturned sheet of coarse sandpaper on a level surface (Figure 8).

8. Finally, cut a rectangular piece $17^{3}/8$" × $8^{1}/2$" from a thin, flexible sheet of translucent Lexan® to form the lens. Now all the pieces are made and you are ready to assemble the lantern.

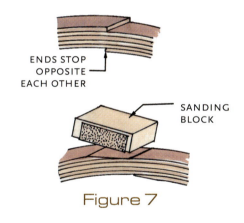

Figure 7

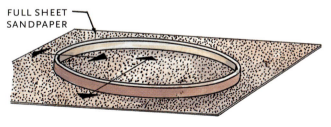

Figure 8

Figure 9

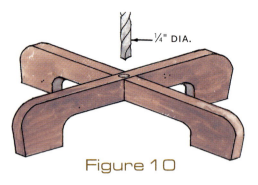

¼" DIA.

Figure 10

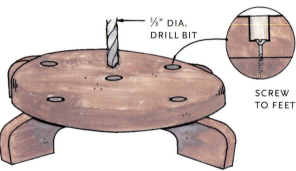

⅜" DIA.
DRILL BIT

SCREW
TO FEET

Figure 11

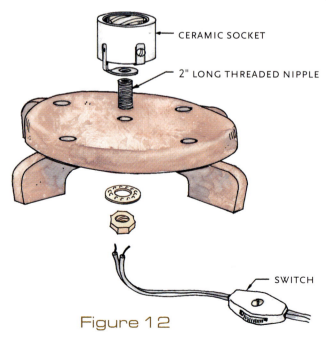

CERAMIC SOCKET

2" LONG THREADED NIPPLE

SWITCH

Figure 12

Assembly

1. Glue the "feet" together with carpenter's glue. Drill a ¼" hole in the center where the feet cross (Figure 10).

2. Drill a ¼" diameter hole in the center of the bottom disc and line this up over the hole in the feet. Glue in place. You can also place four flat-head screws through the disc into the feet by drilling small screw holes through the bottom of each of the four dowel holes made for the upright posts (Figure 11). Enlarge the center hole with a ⅜" diameter bit through the disc and the "feet."

3. Screw a 2" long nipple into the hole in the center of the bottom disc, so it threads itself into the wood. Let it protrude below the underside of the feet enough to allow a lock-washer and nut. With the electrical cord passing through the center hole of the nipple attach the wires to a light socket and screw it onto the nipple (Figure 12).

4. Glue the two remaining discs together to form the top of the lantern. The small one should be centered on the larger one by drilling a ¼" diameter hole through the center of each to register them. The top and can be finished off by gluing a small wooden knob in the center (see Top View and Side View on page 10).

5. This next step is a bit challenging. Glue and assemble the four hoops inside the four uprights at the same time as they are fitted to the bottom and top before the glue dries. This sounds more difficult than it is. Try each upright in its respective hole in the bottom and the top and then number them as you go; that way you won't get caught with a tight fit at a bad moment. The deeper hoop (⁵⁄₁₆") goes on the bot-

tom. Put a thin layer of carpenter's glue around one edge and center it, glue side down, on the bottom disc between the four holes. Next, drop a spot of glue in each of the holes and insert the four uprights with the notches facing the center (Figure 13). Now place the remaining three hoops in their respective notches with a spot of glue in each notch, and bend the Lexan® sheet into a cylinder $8^3/16$" long and slip it down inside the hoops, with the join coinciding with the inside face of one of the uprights. Finally, wrap an elastic band around the uprights to hold the assembly in place at the top.

6. With the Lexan® carefully fitted, put glue on the upper ends of the four uprights and place the top over them. Check the uprights to make sure they are vertical and to make sure that there's no twist in the assembly.

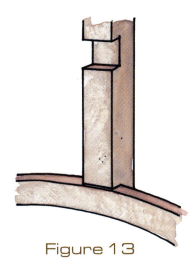

Figure 13

Checklist

At this point it is important to check the following:

a. The inside of the hoops should be flush with the inside face of the uprights (Figure 14, Diagram 1).

b. The edges of the Lexan® should meet exactly, without any gap or overlap, to ensure a tight fit against the inside of the hoops. The Lexan® need not be glued in place.

c. The top of the Lexan® cylinder should be flush with the top of (or just below) the highest loop (Figure 14, Diagram 2).

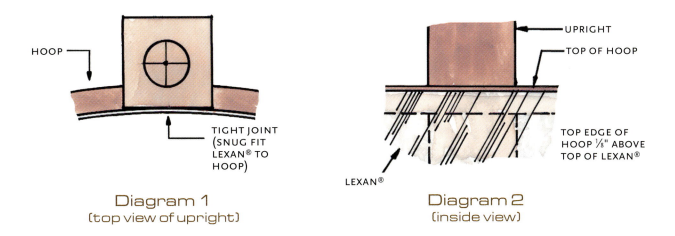

HOOP

TIGHT JOINT (SNUG FIT LEXAN® TO HOOP)

Diagram 1
(top view of upright)

UPRIGHT

TOP OF HOOP

LEXAN®

TOP EDGE OF HOOP ⅛" ABOVE TOP OF LEXAN®

Diagram 2
(inside view)

Figure 14

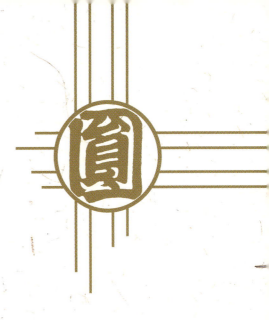

Osaka Table Lantern

This sturdy and attractive lantern has a potential for indoor or outdoor use. The design described is for an indoor lantern. For outdoor use (garden, patio, or either side of an entrance) a weatherproof fixture should be used. In either case a standard incandescent bulb or mini-fluorescent light will work. The lantern can be built as described or made a foot taller (see photo opposite) to accommodate one of the new elongated mini-fluorescent bulbs and used as a floor lantern.

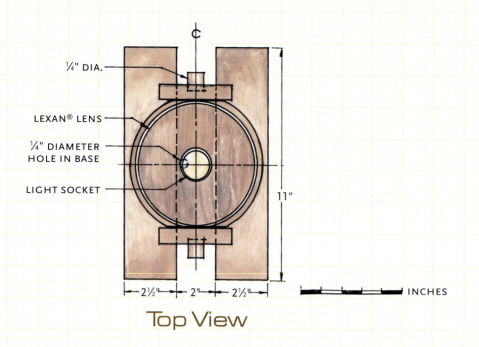

¼" DIA.

LEXAN® LENS

¼" DIAMETER
HOLE IN BASE

LIGHT SOCKET

11"

2½"   2"   2½"

⊢⊢⊢⊢⊢⊣ INCHES

Top View

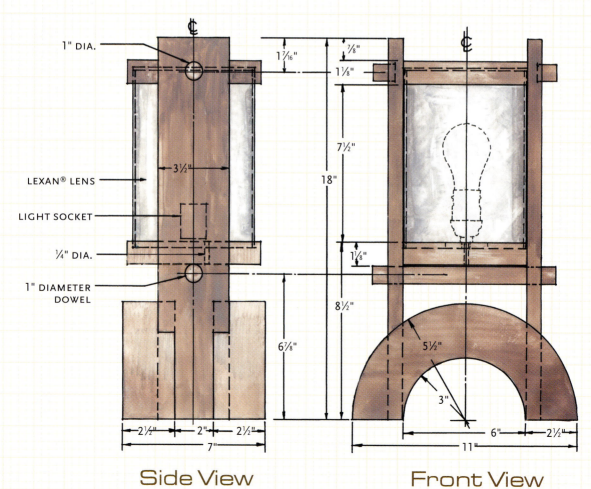

1" DIA.

LEXAN® LENS

LIGHT SOCKET

¼" DIA.

1" DIAMETER
DOWEL

3½"

1 7/16"

1⅛"

7/8"

7½"

18"

1⅛"

8½"

6⅞"

5½"

3"

2½"   2"   2½"

7"

6"   2½"

11"

Side View   ## Front View

Method

1. The first step is to glue up a $2^1/2$" thick panel a minimum of 11" square. In most lumber yards you can find one-by-twelve of softwood or hardwood (which will be dressed out at $3/4$" × $11^1/2$"; see sidebar below). If you can't find a one-by-twelve, edge-glue narrower strips of wood to make up an $11^1/2$" wide board. Glue four $11^1/2$" square boards into a block (Figure 1), planing it to get the correct dimensions if necessary. (You can also make a decorative block by laminating layers of veneers between each board.) After the boards are glued together, use a pencil to divide one face of the block in half with the grain. Find the center of that line and using a compass, scribe two circles, 3" and $5^1/2$" in radius. Cut the panel in half along the dividing line, then carefully bandsaw both circles in each half to obtain two arches and two semi-circles. The two arches will be the feet of the lantern (Figure 2).

2. Bandsaw both semi-circles in half lengthways (Figure 3) and glue two of them together as shown in Figure 4 to

Figure 1

Figure 2

Figure 3

Figure 4

Figure 5

Tools
- Bandsaw, tablesaw, and jigsaw
- Drill with $1/4$", $3/8$", and 1" diameter bits
- Router with $1/8$" diameter bit
- Drawing compass
- C-clamps – at least four

Materials
- Feet, top ring, and bottom disk – cut all from an 11" square by $2^1/2$" thick block of wood (or four one-by-twelves of red cedar, maple, cherry, or walnut)
- Top disk – $1/4$" thick $5^1/4$" square of matching wood
- Sides – two $3/4$" thick by $3^1/2$" wide by $7^1/4$" long each of matching wood
- Bottom dowel – 1" diameter by $8^1/8$" long piece of matching wood
- Top dowels – two 1" diameter by $1^1/4$" long pieces of matching wood
- Lens – $1/16$" thick by $8^1/2$" high by 18" long "frosted" Lexan®
- Carpenter's glue – white or yellow
- Electrical light socket with 1" long threaded nipple, eight feet of electrical cord with switch and plug attached

Figure 6

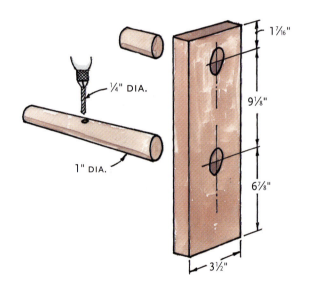

form the bottom disk. With a $1/8$" diameter bit and a guide on the router, cut a $3/16$" deep groove $3/8$" away from the edge as shown in Figure 5. In the center of this disk, drill a $3/8$" diameter hole for the nipple.

3. Take the remaining two semi-circles and bandsaw a pair of $1/4$" thick arches and glue them together to form the top ring as shown in Figure 6.

4. Now make two side panels, $3/4$" thick by $3^1/2$" wide and 18" long, and drill two 1" diameter holes in each located as shown in Figure 7. These panels will fit into slots in the feet on either side of the lens. Cut two vertical $3/4$" deep by $3/4$" wide slots $5^5/8$" apart in each of the two feet.

5. Before gluing the assembly together, drill a $1/4$" diameter hole midway along the side of a 1" diameter dowel, $8^1/8$" long (Figure 7). You will need two more 1" diameter dowels each $1^1/4$" long at the top of the lantern.

6. Where the bottom disk and the ring at the top meet the side panels, each must be $5^1/2$" wide (the distance between the side panels). Cut two flat surfaces on these pieces as shown in Figure 8.

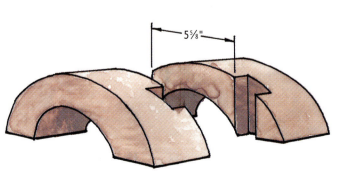

Figure 7

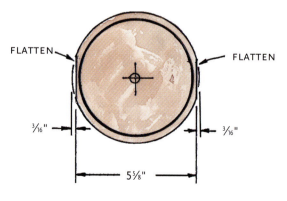

Figure 8

Assembly

1. First, glue the two side panels into their slots in the feet and clamp them in place.

2. Push the long dowel through the lower holes in the side panels, centering the $^1/_4$" hole vertically to allow the electrical cord to exit from the bottom of the disk. There should be $^1/_2$" of the dowel protruding either side. Slip the disc over the dowel and glue all in place.

3. Glue the ring at the top opposite the holes for the two short dowels, leaving $^1/_2$" protruding on each. Both the ring and the disc must be centered and level to hold the Lexan® lens in place.

4. Thread a $^3/_8$" diameter nipple into the hole in the bottom disk and fasten a standard electric light socket over it, threading the electrical cord down through the disk and the dowel. Attach a switch to the cord approximately one foot from the lamp and attach a plug at the end.

6. Cut the lens from $^1/_{16}$" thick frosted Lexan® or similar translucent material so it is $8^1/_2$" high and about 18" long. Bend the material into a tube and slide it down through the ring and into the slot in the bottom disc. Place the joint in the lens opposite one of the side panels.

7. Glue a strip of wood $^1/_8$" × $^3/_8$" vertically inside both side panels as a spacer between between the top ring and the bottom disk as shown in Figure 9. These are spacers to keep the Lexan® from bulging at the joint.

8. To finish off the lantern, bandsaw a $^1/_4$" thick disk of matching wood to fit snugly inside the top ring (Figure 10). Cut a $2^1/_2$" diameter hole in the middle with a jigsaw to allow heat from the bulb to escape.

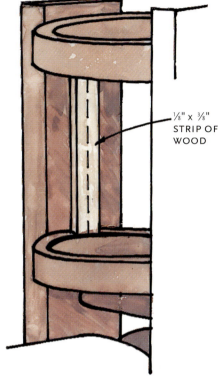

$^1/_8$" × $^3/_8$"
STRIP OF
WOOD

Figure 9

Figure 10

PERSIMMON (kaki) BOX LANTERN

T he box lantern is based on a very old Japanese type originally used to carry a candle in the wind. It consists of a simple square box of thin spruce or fir and a carrying handle. Openings in the sides are covered with shoji to cast the light in a warm glow and the removable lid has finger holes to allow the heat from the bulb to escape. This lantern looks equally well on a desk or as an accent on the floor.

The openings in the sides of the box could all be plain circles. However, I've given the option of including the Japanese symbol or "mon" for equality and peace.

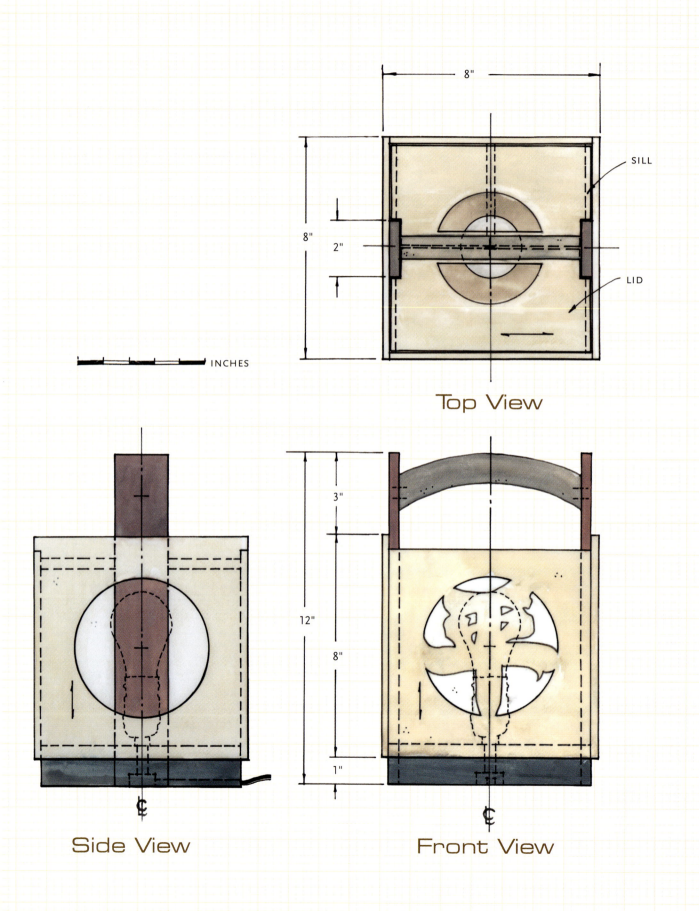

8"

8"

2"

SILL

LID

Top View

INCHES

3"

12"

8"

1"

Side View

Front View

Method

1. From two-by-eight fir or spruce stock make a base 7$\frac{1}{2}$" square. Drill a $\frac{3}{8}$" diameter hole through the center and cut a 2" wide slot $\frac{3}{8}$" deep on two opposite edges of the base as shown in Figure 1. On the underside of the base cut and chisel a $\frac{1}{4}$" square slot from one edge to the hole in the center to lead the electrical cord out from under the lantern. Also, with a $\frac{3}{4}$" diameter drill bit enlarge the center hole on the underside of the base only to a depth of $\frac{1}{2}$" to accommodate a nut and washer.

2. Make two hardwood verticals 2" wide by 12" long by $\frac{3}{8}$" thick. Measure 1$\frac{1}{2}$" down from one end of each vertical and drill a $\frac{3}{8}$" diameter hole $\frac{1}{4}$" deep centered on it. Glue and clamp the uprights into the slots in the base with the end opposite the hole (and with the holes facing each other) flush with the bottom (Figure 2).

3. Using the pattern (Figure 3 – enlarged on a photocopier) cut out the handle from a $\frac{3}{8}$" × 2" × 7" piece of hardwood on a bandsaw. Round the edges with a handplane, a wood rasp, and sandpaper.

4. With $\frac{3}{8}$" diameter dowel centers in place in the two holes in the verticals, spread the verticals enough to

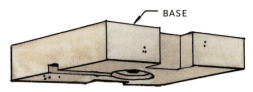

Figure 1

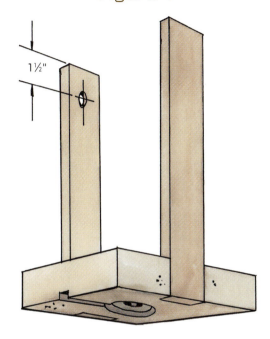

1$\frac{1}{2}$"

Figure 2

Tools	Materials	
• Tablesaw, bandsaw, and jigsaw	• Base – hard- or softwood, two-by-eight 7$\frac{1}{2}$" long	• Shoji – mulberry paper: five pieces 6$\frac{1}{2}$" square (you could also use one of the handmade papers available at art supply stores)
• Drill with $\frac{3}{8}$" and $\frac{3}{4}$" twist drill bits	• Verticals – two hardwood pieces 2" × $\frac{1}{4}$" × 12" long each	
• Handplane	• Handle – cut from one hardwood piece $\frac{3}{4}$" × 2 $\frac{1}{4}$" × 7" long	• Carpenter's glue – white or yellow
• Chisel – $\frac{1}{4}$" wide		
• Wood rasp	• Sides – $\frac{1}{4}$" thick spruce or fir (or plywood): two pieces 8" × 8" and two pieces 7$\frac{1}{2}$" × 7 $\frac{5}{8}$"	• Standard electric lamp socket with a 2" long threaded nipple ($\frac{3}{8}$" diameter), six feet of 18 ga. lamp cord with a switch and a plug
• Two bar clamps		
• Dowel-centering points		
• Bench square	• Lid – $\frac{1}{4}$" thick spruce or fir 7$\frac{1}{2}$" × 7$\frac{1}{2}$"	
• Drawing compass		• Felt – 7" × 7"
• Utility knife and/or scissors	• Lid supports – four $\frac{3}{8}$" square fir 2$\frac{3}{4}$" long each	
• Atomizer		

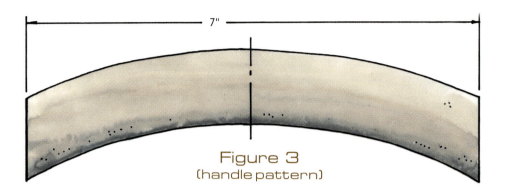

Figure 3
(handle pattern)

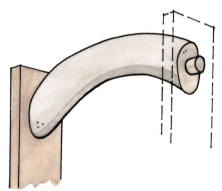

Figure 4

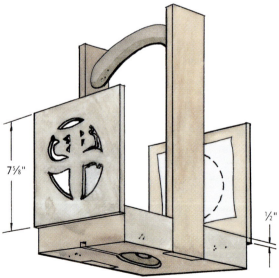

Figure 5

lower the handle between them until the top of the curve is even with the tops of the verticals. Squeeze the verticals together to mark the center for $3/8$" diameter by $1/4$" deep holes in each end of the handle. Drill these holes and glue a $1/2$" long $3/8$" diameter dowel in each of them (Figure 4). With glue on the dowels, spread the verticals again and clamp the handle in place between them.

5. From $1/4$" thick spruce or fir cut two pieces 8" by 8" and two pieces $7^1/2$" by $7^5/8$" for the sides of the box. Find the center of one face of each piece and using a drawing compass, scribe a 3" radius circle on each. On page 27 there is a pattern for a Japanese "mon" representing equality and peace (Figure 8). If you wish to use this design, enlarge the pattern on a photocopier until it is 6" in diameter and transfer it to each of the two $7^1/2$" by $7^5/8$" side pieces. Drill starter-holes within the areas to be removed and cut them out with a scroll saw. Sand the four sides thoroughly.

6. Cut out four $6^1/2$" square sheets of shoji (mulberry paper) and glue them on the back of each side piece, covering the holes. With an atomizer spray water over the paper and set them aside to dry.

7. Glue and clamp the two smaller sides to the base $1/2$" down from the top on the sides opposite those with the verticals attached. Note that the $7^1/2$" dimension on each side must match that dimension on the base with the edges flush (Figure 5).

8. Glue and clamp the remaining sides to the base and to the edges of the first sides. Note that the bottom of all sides should be flush and even with each other all the way around; also, the tops of the larger (8" sq.) sides will be ³/₈" above the other two (see front view on page 24).

9. From ¹/₄" thick spruce or fir cut a 7¹/₂" square lid. Find the center of one face and scribe a 2" radius circle on it. Bisect the circle with a 1" wide strip drawn parallel with the grain. Drill starter-holes within the two semi-circles and cut out the "finger holes" with a jigsaw (refer to Figure 6). Cut two notches ³/₈" by 2" as shown to fit around the verticals and "trim" the edges of the lid with sandpaper until it fits inside the box.

10. Cut four pieces of softwood ³/₈" square by 2³/₄" long and glue them inside the box on either side of the verticals to support the lid (¹/₄" below the top of the short sides) as shown in Figure 7.

11. Screw a 2" long threaded nipple to the lower half of a standard lamp socket then screw it through the center hole in the base. Fasten a nut and washer to the underside. Lead one end of the 18 ga. lamp cord up through the nipple, separate the wires for about 3", and tie a reefknot in it. Attach the ends of the wires to the lamp socket proper, slip the cardboard tube and the brass sleeve over it, then snap the assembly in place on the lower half of the socket. Lead the cord out through the slot and glue a layer of felt on the base. Attach a plug to the end of the cord and a switch about one foot away from the lantern.

12. Finish the wood on the lantern with oil or varnish.

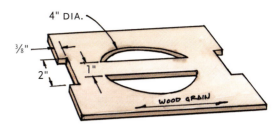

Figure 6

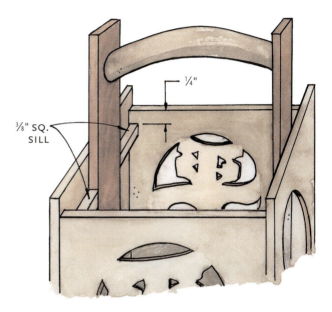

Figure 7

Figure 8
(pattern — "equality and peace")

Tea Berry (Chanomi) Double Shade Box Lantern

This unusual lantern consists of a wood-framed paper box originally intended for carrying a candle in the wind and a separate wooden box with rather small openings in which to put the lantern to reduce the light emitted. Similar to the previous project, this lantern is a glowing cube with a handle, but this one can sit on a table on its own or be attached to the top of the outer box to give it some extra height when placed on the floor. To shade the lantern, the outer box is placed over it with the handle passing through a slot in the top.

Again I have shown the Japanese "mon" for equality and peace.

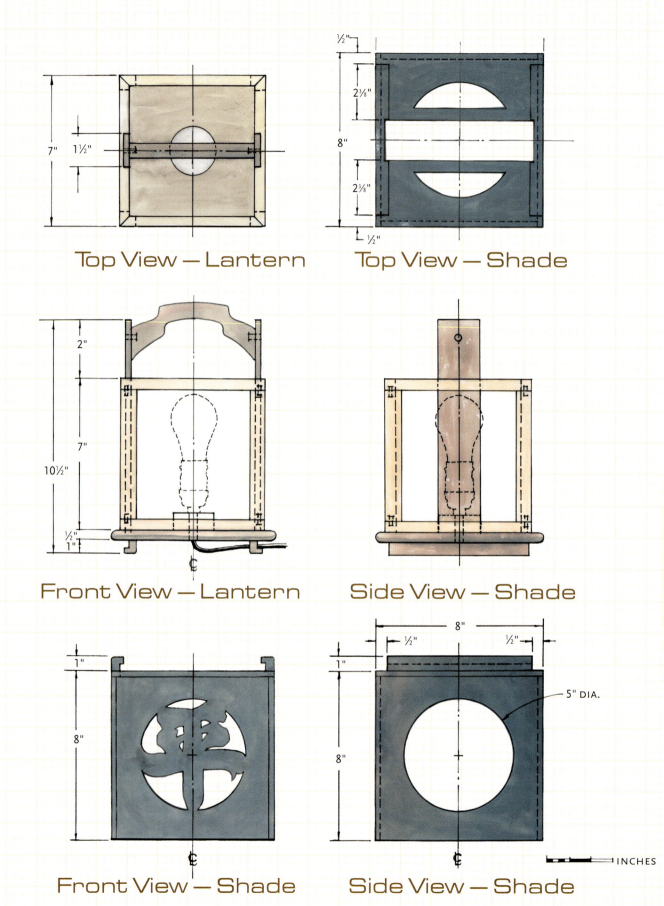

Top View — Lantern

Top View — Shade

Front View — Lantern

Side View — Shade

Front View — Shade

Side View — Shade

INCHES

Method

1. From ¹/₂" thick plywood cut out a 7" square. From ¹/₂" square hardwood stock (cherry, walnut, maple, etc.) cut four trim pieces each 8" long. Mitre the ends on a tablesaw (45 degrees) and glue them in place around the edges of the plywood base using one of the clamping methods suggested on page 51 (Morning Glory Lantern). When the glue has dried, plane and sand them round as shown in the front and side views.

2. From ³/₄" fir or hardwood stock, make a 2" square socket-mounting block, center it on the base, and glue it in place. Find the center and drill a ³/₈" diameter hole through the block and the base (Figure 1).

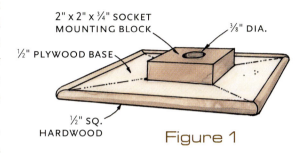

2" x 2" x ¾" SOCKET MOUNTING BLOCK

⅜" DIA.

½" PLYWOOD BASE

½" SQ. HARDWOOD

Figure 1

Tools

- Tablesaw, bandsaw, and jigsaw
- Drill with ⅛", ¼", and ⅜" twist drill bits
- Handplane
- Wood rasp
- Two bar clamps and a picture frame clamp (or something similar)
- Dowel-centering points
- Bench square
- Drawing compass
- Utility knife and/or scissors
- Atomizer

Materials

- Base – ½" thick birch or fir plywood 7" square
- Base trim – four pieces of ½" square hardwood (cherry, walnut, etc.) 8" long each
- Base runners – two pieces of hardwood ½" by 1" by 7" long each
- Socket mounting block – ¾" thick fir or hardwood 2" square
- Lantern box frame – eight pieces ½" square hardwood 7" long each and four pieces ¾" square hardwood 6" long each
- Verticals – two hardwood pieces 1½" × ½" × 9¾" long each
- Handle – cut from one hardwood piece ½" × 1¼" × 6" long
- Shade sides – ¼" thick plywood or hardboard: two pieces 8" × 7¾" and two pieces 7½" × 7¾"
- Shade top – ¼" thick plywood or hardboard: 8" × 8"
- Shade runners – two pieces of hardwood ½" by ¾" by 7" long each
- Shoji – mulberry paper: four pieces 6½" square each (you could also use one of the handmade papers available at art supply stores)
- Dowels – eight ⅛" diameter hardwood ¼" long each (bamboo skewers work well for this)
- Two ¼" diameter hardwood ¾" long each
- Carpenter's glue – white or yellow
- Enamel or lacquer (paint) – one pint
- Standard electric lamp socket with a 1¼" long threaded nipple (⅜" diameter), six feet of 18 ga. lamp cord with a switch and a plug

3. The lantern box is made up of a top and a bottom frame (from $1/2$" square hardwood stock) joined by four $3/4$" square corner posts $6 1/2$" long each. Cut eight $1/2$" square pieces 7" long with mitred ends (45 degrees) and glue together two frames using picture frame clamps (Figure 2).

4. Cut four corner-posts with $1/4$" square rabbets along the inside edges as shown in Figure 3 then drill $1/8$" diameter holes $1/8$" deep into each end. At each corner of the frames, drill corresponding holes as shown in Figure 4. With the rabbets facing inward and a $1/8$" diameter dowel glued into

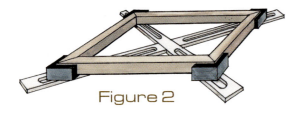

Figure 2

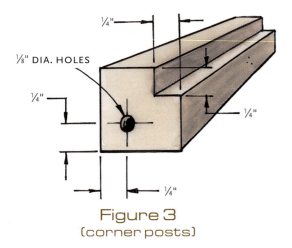

$1/8$" DIA. HOLES

Figure 3
(corner posts)

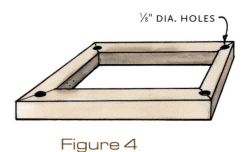

$1/8$" DIA. HOLES

Figure 4

the ends of each corner post, glue the lantern box assembly together as shown in Figure 5. Centered on the inside of two opposite sides of the top and bottom frames, cut $1 1/2$" wide notches $1/4$" deep (Figure 5).

5. Make two hardwood verticals $1 1/2$" wide by $1/2$" thick by $9 3/4$"long. In one face of each vertical,

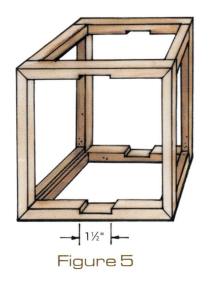

$1 1/2$"

Figure 5

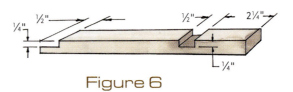

$1/2$" $1/2$" $2 1/4$"

$1/4$"

$1/4$"

Figure 6

measure down 2$^1/_4$" and from there cut a $^1/_2$" dado $^1/_4$" deep. At the other end, on the same face of each vertical, cut a $^1/_4$" by $^1/_2$" rabbet (Figure 6). Glue and clamp the 1$^1/_2$" wide uprights in place centered in opposite sides of the framed box flush with the bottom frame and fitted into the notches in the top frame (Figure 7).

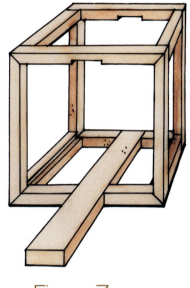

Figure 7

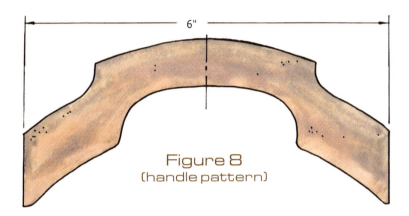

Figure 8
(handle pattern)

6. Using the pattern (Figure 8 – enlarged on a photocopier) cut out the handle from a $^1/_2$" × 1$^1/_4$" × 6" piece of hardwood on a bandsaw. Round the edges with a handplane, a wood rasp, and sandpaper.

7. Clamp the handle centered between the two verticals with the top of the arch level with the tops of the verticals, measure $^3/_4$" down from the tops, and drill $^1/_4$" diameter holes through the verticals into the handle. With glue on the ends of the handle, glue two $^1/_4$" diameter dowels into the holes and clamp the assembly together until the glue has dried (Figure 9). Trim the ends of the dowels flush with the verticals.

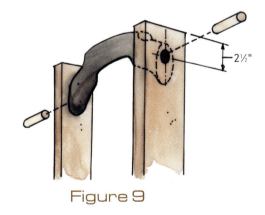

Figure 9

8. From ½" by 1" hardwood, cut two lengths 7" long each for runners (Figure 10). Cut a ¼" square rabbet along one edge of both pieces and glue them in place underneath the lantern with the inside edges 1⅜" in from the outside edge of the base (Figure 11).

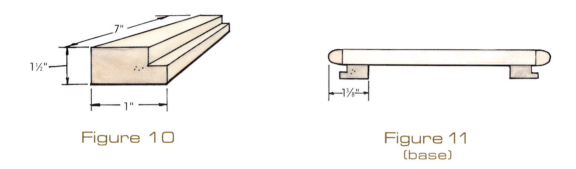

Figure 10

Figure 11
(base)

9. Cut out four 6½" square sheets of shoji (mulberry paper) and glue them inside the lantern frame. With an atomizer spray water over the paper and set them aside to dry.

10. Screw a 1½" long threaded nipple to the lower half of a standard lamp socket then screw it through the center hole in the base. Fasten a nut and washer to the underside. Lead one end of the 18 ga. lamp cord up through the nipple, separate the wires for about 3", and tie a reefknot in it. Attach the ends of the wires to the lamp socket proper, slip the cardboard tube and the brass sleeve over it, then snap the assembly in place on the lower half of the socket. Attach a plug to the end of the cord and a switch about one foot away from the lantern (see details in the Appendix).

11. Finish the wood on the lantern with oil or varnish.

12. To make the shade (from ¼" thick plywood or hardboard), cut out two sides 8" x 7¾", two sides 7½" x 7¾" and a top 8" × 8". Locate the center of each side and, with a drawing compass, scribe a 5" diameter circle; with a jigsaw, cut full circles out of the smaller of the two sides. Like the previous project (the Persimmon" Box Lantern), I have shown a Japanese "mon" on the front and back of this lantern, representing equality and peace. Refer

to the pattern on page 27 (Figure 8) and enlarge it to 5" diameter on a photocopier. Transfer the design to the center of the two larger sides and cut them out with a jigsaw or scroll saw. In the center of the top, scribe a 4" diameter circle and lay out a slot 1³/4" wide by 7" long. Parallel to the slot, 1/2" away from either side of it, draw lines crossing the circle (see Figure 12) Cut out the slot and the two half-circles with a jigsaw.

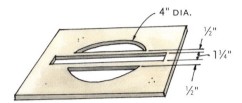

Figure 12

13. Glue the sides together to form an 8" square box then glue the top to the sides with the full circles opposite the verticals.

14. From 1/2" square hardwood, cut two lengths 7" long each for runners. Cut a 1/8" × 1/4" rabbet along one edge of both pieces and glue them to the top of the box, flush with the edges opposite the ends of the slot as shown in Figure 13 below.

15. Sand the box thoroughly then paint it inside and out with several coats of enamel or lacquer. Black was a traditional color but you may want to select a different color to compliment your room's decor.

Figure 13

Mulberry (Kaji) Lantern

This design is related to the last two designs in that it was an old style of lantern for carrying a candle: in this case, a very tall one. Rather than being a wooden box, however, the sides are made with a stiff shoji to allow the light to radiate from a much larger surface; in fact, having a minimal wooden frame, the whole lantern seems to glow. The shoji used is a modern plasticized paper rigid enough to stand on its own without a frame at the corners. Otherwise it is similar to the Persimmon Lantern with a handle and an access lid at the top.

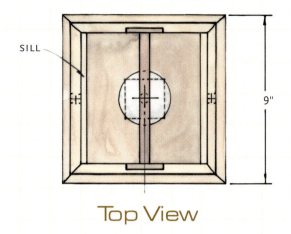

SILL

9"

Top View

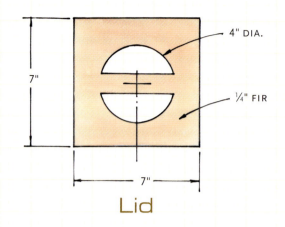

4" DIA.

7"

¼" FIR

7"

Lid

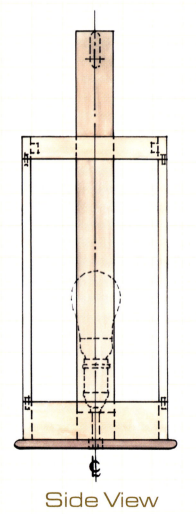

Side View

INCHES

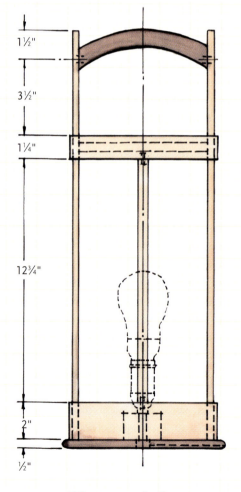

1½"

3½"

1¼"

12¾"

2"

½"

Front View

Method

1. From ¹/₂" thick birch or fir plywood cut out an 8" square, find the center, and drill a ³/₄" diameter hole through it. From ¹/₂" square hardwood stock (cherry, walnut, maple, etc.) cut four trim pieces each 9" long. Mitre the ends on a tablesaw (45 degrees) and glue them in place around the edges of the plywood base using one of the clamping methods suggested on page 51 (Morning Glory lantern). When the glue has dried, plane and sand them round as shown in the front and side views. On the underside of the base cut and chisel a ¹/₄" square slot from one edge to the hole in the center to lead the electrical cord out from under the lantern (Figure 1).

2. From 1¹/₂" fir or hardwood stock, make a 2" square socket-mounting block. Find the center and drill a ³/₈" diameter hole through it. Center this block over the hole in the base and glue it in place (Figure 2).

3. From ¹/₂" fir cut four 2" wide pieces 8" long to make the bottom frame. Mitre the ends of each piece across the ¹/₂" dimension as shown in Figure 3. On two of these pieces cut a ¹/₄" × 2" dado on the inside

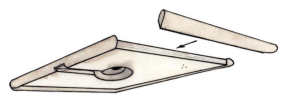

Figure 1
(underside of base)

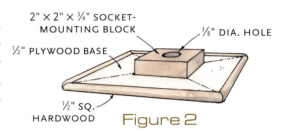

2" × 2" × ³/₄" SOCKET-
MOUNTING BLOCK
³/₈" DIA. HOLE
¹/₂" PLYWOOD BASE
¹/₂" SQ.
HARDWOOD **Figure 2**

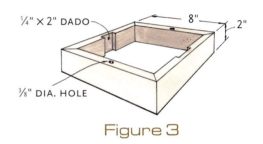

¹/₄" × 2" DADO
8"
2"
³/₈" DIA. HOLE

Figure 3

Tools

- Tablesaw, bandsaw, and jigsaw
- Drill with ³/₈" and ³/₄" twist drill bits
- Handplane
- Chisel – ¹/₄" wide
- Wood rasp
- Two barclamps and one or more strap-clamps
- Dowel-centering points
- Bench square
- Utility knife and/or scissors

Materials

- Base – ¹/₂" plywood 8" square with four hardwood trim pieces ¹/₂" square by 9" long

- Lamp socket mounting block – 2" × 2" × 1¹/₂" thick hard- or softwood
- Bottom frame – four softwood pieces ¹/₂" × 2" × 8" long each
- Top frame – four softwood pieces ¹/₂" × 1¹/₄" × 8" long each
- Handle verticals – two hardwood pieces ¹/₄" × 2¹/₂" × 2¹/₂" long each
- Vertical bars – two softwood pieces ¹/₂" square × 12³/₄" long each
- Handle – cut from one hardwood piece ³/₄" × 2¹/₄" × 6³/₄" long

- Lid – ¹/₄" thick softwood 7" square
- Lid supports – two ¹/₂" × ¹³/₁₆" × 7" long each
- Shoji – two sheets of plasticized paper 12" × 14" each
- Carpenter's glue – white or yellow
- Contact cement
- Felt – 7¹/₂" × 7¹/₂"
- Standard electric lamp socket with a 2" long threaded nipple (³/₈" diameter), six feet of 18 ga. lamp cord with a switch and plug

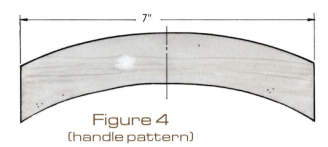

Figure 4
(handle pattern)

7"

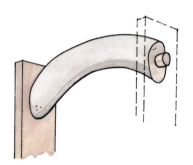

Figure 5

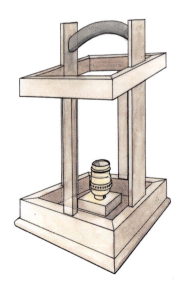

Figure 6

edge. On the other two pieces drill $3/8$" diameter holes $1/4$" deep in the center of the top edge. Glue the four bottom frame pieces together at the corners using one or more strap clamps or one of the methods described on page 51 (Morning Glory lantern). Note that the dadoes must be facing each other on opposite sides. When the glue has dried, glue and clamp the frame onto the base.

4. Make two $1/4$" × 2" hardwood handle verticals $21^1/2$" long each. Measure $1^1/2$" down from one end of each piece and drill a $3/8$" diameter hole $1/4$" deep centered on it. Glue and clamp the verticals into the dadoes in the bottom frame with the holes facing each other.

5. Using the pattern (Figure 4 – enlarged on a photocopier) cut out the handle from a $3/8$" × 2" × 7" piece of hardwood on a bandsaw. Round the edges with a handplane, a wood rasp, and sandpaper.

6. With $3/8$" diameter dowel centers in place in the two holes in the verticals, spread the verticals enough to lower the handle between them until the top of the curve is even with the tops of the verticals. Squeeze the verticals together to mark the center for $3/8$" diameter by $1/4$" deep holes in each end of the handle. Drill these holes and glue a $1/2$" long $3/8$" diameter dowel in each of them (Figure 5). With glue on the dowels, spread the verticals again and clamp the handle in place between them.

7. From $1/2$" square fir cut two pieces $12^3/4$" long to make the vertical bars. Drill a $3/8$" diameter hole $1/4$" deep at each end. Glue $1/2$" long $3/8$" dowels into these holes.

8. From $1/2$" fir cut four $1^1/4$" wide pieces 8" long to make the top frame. Mitre the ends of each piece across the $1/2$" dimension. On two of these pieces cut a $1/4$" × 2" dado on the inside edge. On the other two pieces drill $3/8$" diameter holes $1/4$" deep in the center of the bottom edge. Glue the four top frame pieces together at the corners using the same clamping method used for the bottom frames. Note that the dadoes must be facing each other on opposite sides, as in the bottom frames.

9. Glue the two vertical bars in place on the bottom frame then glue and clamp the top frame in place on the handle verticals and over the bars (Figure 6).

10. Cut out two sheets of shoji (plasticized paper) 12" by 14". Measure 2¹/₂" in from either side (across the 12" dimension) and fold two sides as shown in Figure 7. Fit the shoji in place inside the lantern and mark where its edges are as a guide to gluing. Apply contact cement around the inside edges of the openings in the lantern. Apply contact cement in a ¹/₄" wide band around the outside edges of the shoji as well as down the center of the 7" wide panel (Figure 8).When the cement is tacky (not sticky), glue the shoji in place inside the lantern.

11. From ¹/₄" thick fir cut a 7" square lid. Find the center of one face and scribe a 2" radius circle on it. Bisect the circle with a 1" wide strip drawn parallel with the grain. Drill starter-holes within the two semi-circles and cut out the "finger holes" with a jigsaw (refer to Figure 9). Trim the edges of the lid with sandpaper until it fits inside the box.

12. From ¹/₂" × ³/₁₆" fir, cut two pieces 7" long for lid supports. With glue on one ³/₁₆" edge, clamp them in place inside the lantern flush with the bottom edge of the top frame opposite the handle verticals (Figure 10).

13. Screw a 2" long threaded nipple to the lower half of a standard lamp socket then screw it through the center hole in the base. Fasten a nut and washer to the underside. Lead one end of the 18 ga. lamp cord up through the nipple, separate the wires for about 3", and tie a reefknot in it. Attach the ends of the wires to the lamp socket proper, slip the cardboard tube and the brass sleeve over it, then snap the assembly in place on the lower half of the socket. Lead the cord out through the slot and glue a layer of felt on the base. Attach a plug to the end of the cord and a switch about one foot away from the lantern.

14. Finish the wood on the lantern with oil or varnish.

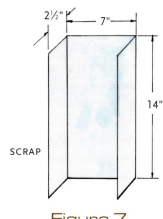

2½" 7"

14"

SCRAP

Figure 7

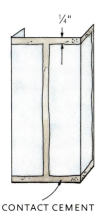

¼"

CONTACT CEMENT

Figure 8

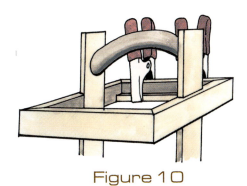

Figure 10

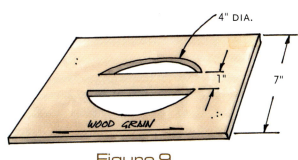

4" DIA.

1"

7"

WOOD GRAIN

Figure 9

PEONY (BOTAN) TABLE LANTERN

This variation of the Mulberry lantern is round rather than square. Its similarities, however, include a handle and an access lid at the top. Being round, it also allows for a minimal wooden frame, maximizing the light emission. Like the first project in this book, the Cherry Blossom, this lantern utilizes a Lexan® lens.

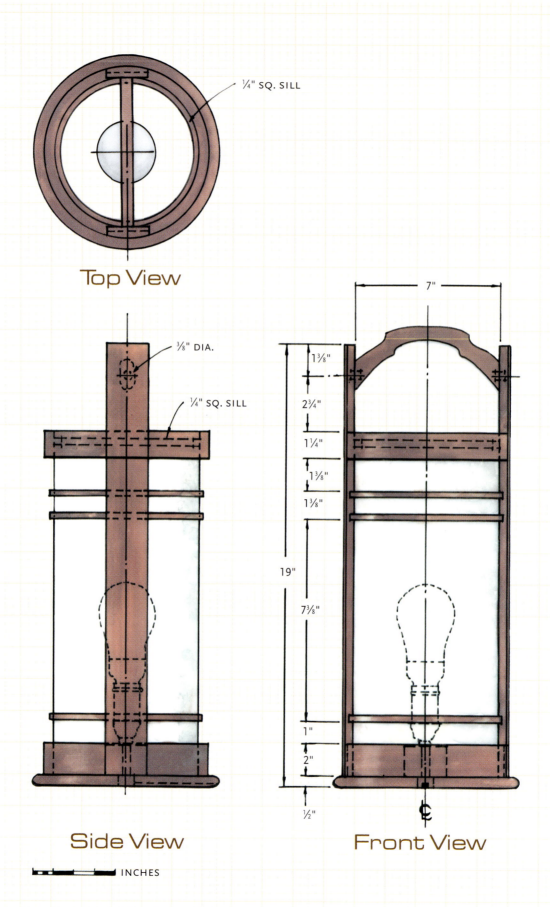

Top View

¼" SQ. SILL

⅜" DIA.

¼" SQ. SILL

7"

1⅜"

2¾"

1¼"

1⅜"

1⅜"

19"

7⅜"

1"

2"

½"

Side View

Front View

INCHES

Method

1. To make the base, scribe a 9" diameter circle on ½" hardwood (cherry, walnut, maple, etc.) with a drawing compass. Bandsaw the disc, drill a ¾" diameter hole through the center, and round both edges with a wood rasp and sandpaper. Saw and chisel a ¼" square slot from one edge to the center hole.

2. From 1½" fir or hardwood stock, make a 2" square socket-mounting block. Find the center and drill a ⅜" diameter hole through it. Center this block over the hole in the 9" diameter disc and glue it in place (Figure 1).

3. To make the top and bottom rings, scribe two sets of concentric circles (8" and 7") on a 1¼" thick piece of hardwood for the top and a 2" thick piece for the bottom. Bandsaw the two discs then cut them exactly in half to facilitate bandsawing the 7" diameter circles in the center. Glue them together again and cut ¼" × 2" wide notches on the outside edges of the discs centered on the sawcuts (Figure 2). Center the bottom ring over the base and glue and clamp it in place.

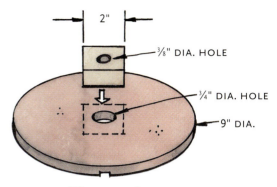

Figure 1

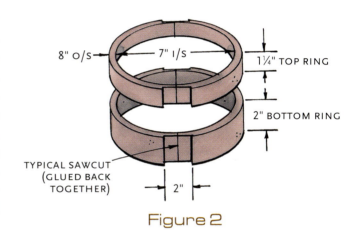

Figure 2

Tools	Materials	
• Tablesaw, bandsaw, jigsaw, and a small hand crosscut saw	• Base – 9" diameter hardwood disc ½" thick	• Handle – cut from one hardwood piece ¾" × 2¼" × 6¾" long
• Drill with ⅜" and ½" bits	• Lamp socket mounting block – 2" × 2" × 1½" thick hard- or softwood	• Hardwood edgebanding – ¾" by 6 feet
• Handplane	• Bottom frame – ½" × 1½" × 8" diameter (outside) hardwood	• Thin Lexan® sheet – 14" × 20"
• Chisel – ¼" wide	• Top frame – ½" × 1¼" × 8" diameter (outside) hardwood	• Carpenter's glue – white or yellow
• Bench square	• Verticals – two hardwood pieces ½" × 2" × 20" long each	• Contact cement
• Wood rasp	• Lid – ¼" thick softwood 7" diameter	• Standard electric lamp socket with a 2" long threaded nipple (⅜ diameter), six feet of 18 ga. lamp cord with a switch and plug
• Two barclamps and one or more spring clamps		
• Dowel-centering points		
• Drawing compass		
• Utility knife and/or scissors		
• Clothes iron		

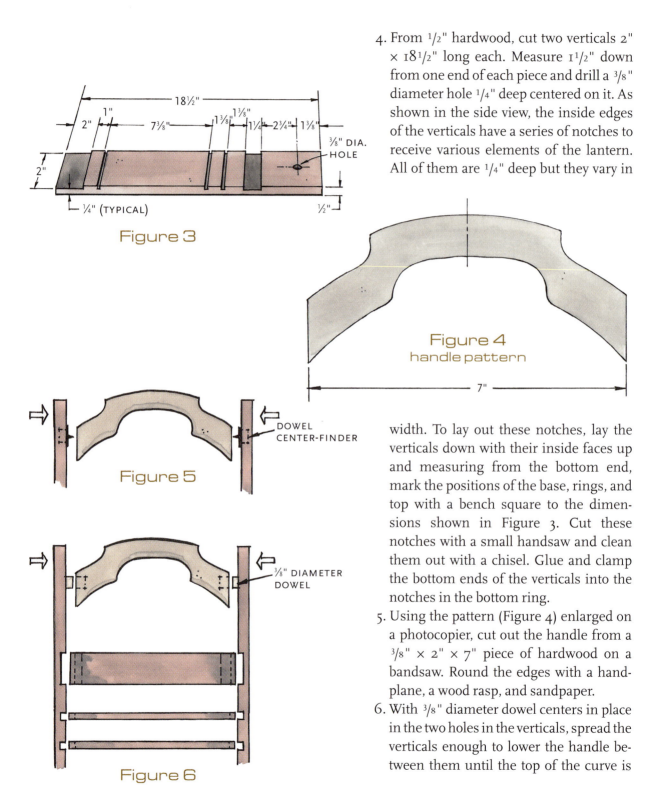

Figure 3

Figure 4
handle pattern

Figure 5
DOWEL
CENTER-FINDER

Figure 6
3/8" DIAMETER
DOWEL

4. From 1/2" hardwood, cut two verticals 2" × 181/2" long each. Measure 11/2" down from one end of each piece and drill a 3/8" diameter hole 1/4" deep centered on it. As shown in the side view, the inside edges of the verticals have a series of notches to receive various elements of the lantern. All of them are 1/4" deep but they vary in width. To lay out these notches, lay the verticals down with their inside faces up and measuring from the bottom end, mark the positions of the base, rings, and top with a bench square to the dimensions shown in Figure 3. Cut these notches with a small handsaw and clean them out with a chisel. Glue and clamp the bottom ends of the verticals into the notches in the bottom ring.

5. Using the pattern (Figure 4) enlarged on a photocopier, cut out the handle from a 3/8" × 2" × 7" piece of hardwood on a bandsaw. Round the edges with a handplane, a wood rasp, and sandpaper.

6. With 3/8" diameter dowel centers in place in the two holes in the verticals, spread the verticals enough to lower the handle between them until the top of the curve is

even with the tops of the verticals. Squeeze the verticals together to mark the center for $3/8$" diameter by $1/4$" deep holes in each end of the handle (Figure 5). Drill these holes and glue a $1/2$" long $3/8$" diameter dowel in each of them. With glue on the dowels, spread the verticals again and clamp the handle in place between them. At the same time, glue the top ring in place in the verticals (Figure 6).

7. By the method described on pages 12 and 13 of the first project and using hardwood edgebanding, make three wooden rings $1/4$" wide and no more than $1/4$" thick. The rings must have an inside diameter of 7". Glue the rings in place in their appropriate notches between the verticals being sure that they are concentric.

8. Screw a 2" long threaded nipple to the lower half of a standard lamp socket then screw it through the hole in the socket mounting block. Fasten a nut and washer to the underside. Lead one end of the 18 ga. lamp cord up through the nipple, separate the wires for about 3", and tie a reefknot in it. Attach the ends of the wires to the lamp socket proper, slip the cardboard tube and the brass sleeve over it, then snap the assembly in place on the lower half of the socket. Lead the cord out through the slot and glue an 8" diameter disc of felt on the base (Figure 7). Attach a plug to the end of the cord and a switch about one foot away from the lantern.

9. Cut out a sheet of Lexan® 20" by 14". Fit the Lexan® in place inside the lantern through the top, lining up the join behind one of the verticals. Because the material is so stiff, it is not necessary to glue it in place. (Note: To ensure a perfect fit of the Lexan®, use a method of trial and error with a sheet of stiff paper and use it as a pattern.)

10. On $1/4$" thick fir scribe concentric circles 7" and 4" in diameter. Bisect the smaller circle with a 1" wide strip drawn parallel with the grain. Drill starter-holes within the two semi-circles and cut out the "finger holes" with a jigsaw (refer to Figure 8). Bandsaw the outer circle and "trim" the edges with sandpaper until it fits inside the box as a lid. To support the lid, make another $1/4$" wide ring with edgebanding 7" outside diameter and glue it inside the top ring $3/8$" down to form a sill.

11. Finish the wood on the lantern with oil or varnish.

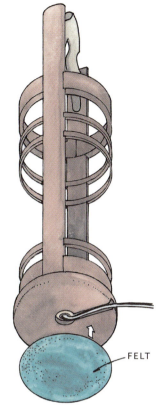

FELT

Figure 7

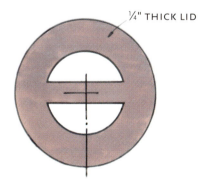

$1/4$" THICK LID

Figure 8

MORNING GLORY (ASAGO) TABLE LANTERN

This lamp combines the delicate structure of a paper lantern with heavier architectural elements for a very pleasing balance of forms. The square legs enclosing the lantern also support a solid wood top. This top with its mitered corners requires a bit of skill to build, but with accurate measuring and cutting you will enjoy making this lamp.

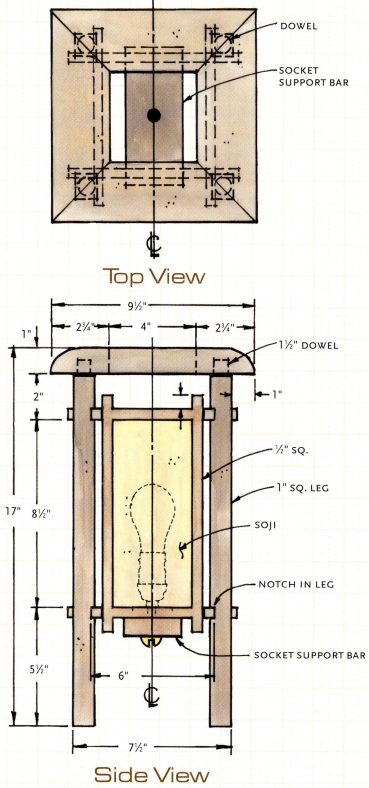

DOWEL

SOCKET
SUPPORT BAR

Top View

9½"

2¾"   4"   2¾"

1"

1½" DOWEL

2"

1"

½" SQ.

1" SQ. LEG

17"   8½"

SOJI

NOTCH IN LEG

SOCKET SUPPORT BAR

5½"

6"

7½"

Side View
(all four sides the same)

INCHES

Method

1. Cut four pieces of 1" × 2$\frac{1}{2}$" × 9$\frac{1}{2}$" hardwood with a 45 degree angle at each end to make a top with mitered corners. With a tablesaw, cut $\frac{1}{4}$" wide × $\frac{1}{4}$" deep slots in the mitred faces which stop before they cut through the outside corners. Make four $\frac{1}{4}$" × $\frac{1}{2}$" splines (Figure 1).

2. With the splines curved in place and glue on the mitred faces, clamp the four sides of the top together simultaneously. There are several methods for clamping, as shown in Figure 2:

   Diagram A – two bar- or pipe-clamps

   Diagram B – a single strap-clamp with a ratchet tightener

   Diagram C – a commercially available picture frame clamp

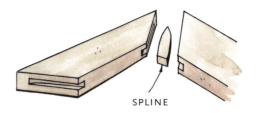

SPLINE

Figure 1

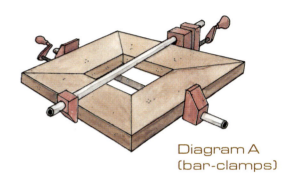

**Diagram A
(bar-clamps)**

Figure 2

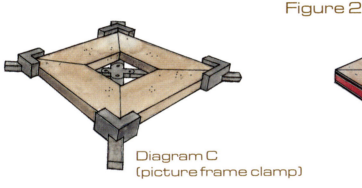

**Diagram C
(picture frame clamp)**

**Diagram B
(strap clamp)**

Tools
- Tablesaw and small crosscut saw
- Drill with $\frac{3}{8}$" and $\frac{1}{2}$" diameter bits
- Chisel – $\frac{1}{2}$" wide
- Utility knife
- A strap-clamp or two bar- or pipe-clamps, or a picture frame clamp
- Screwdriver
- Dowel-centering points
- Set square
- Atomizer
- Builder's level

Materials
- Top – four pieces of 1" × 2$\frac{3}{4}$" × 9$\frac{1}{2}$" long hardwood
- Legs – four legs each 1" square × 16" long hardwood
- Screen frames – sixteen $\frac{1}{2}$" square pieces from two-by-five hardwood, 11" long
- Mounting block – 1" × 3" × 6" long hardwood
- Hardwood dowel – $\frac{1}{2}$" diameter × 8" long
- Rice paper (or other decorative handmade paper) – 10" × 24"
- Two brass roundhead screws
- Electric light socket with 1" long threaded nipple and a minimum six-foot length of electrical wire with switch and plug
- Carpenter's glue – white or yellow

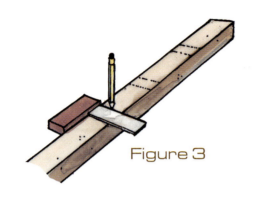

Figure 3

Figure 4

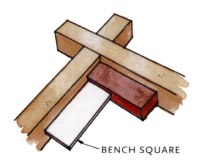

BENCH SQUARE

Figure 5

3. Cut four 1" square hardwood legs, each 16" long and sand them ready for finishing.

4. The body of the lantern consists of four papered wood-framed screens joined to form a square box. Make the four screens separately from 1/2" square lap-jointed pieces all cut from two-by-six hardwood. For each screen, cut two pieces, 8" long and two pieces, 10" long.

5. On each piece, mark out the location of each 1/4" deep notch (see Figure 3) used for the lap joint using a set square. As shown in Figure 4, cut each notch carefully with a fine handsaw and a sharp chisel. Note: The notches in the two 8" long pieces are 1 1/2" from each end and the notches in the two 10" long pieces are 1/2" from each end.

6. Press-fit all the lap joints together at once (without glue) as a trial run. Use a chisel to clean up or enlarge any notch showing signs of resistance until the frame lies flat and each corner is at a perfect ninety degrees (Figure 5). Re-assemble the frame with a thin layer of glue in each joint and place a piece of plywood over the frame with several weights on top to hold it in place until the glue has dried. Repeat this process with the other three frames.

7. Carefully sand and finish each frame with oil, wax, or varnish, leaving the inside face bare so the paper can be glued to it.

8. Thin some carpenter's glue with water and spread it carefully over the back of each piece of the frame. Lay a sheet of mulberry paper on the frame, being careful to avoid wrinkles or creases. Once the glue has dried, mist water over both sides of the paper with an atomizer to shrink it. While the paper dries, lay the frame upside down on a flat surface with a weight at each corner (Figure 6).

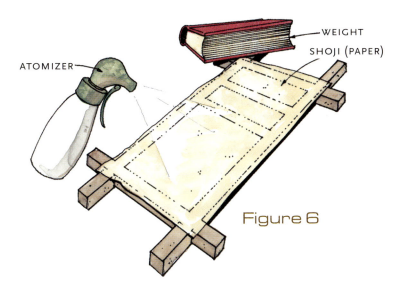

Figure 6

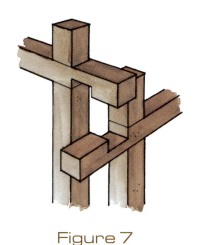

Figure 7

9. Join the four screens together in a square box shape with lap joints in the top and bottom cross pieces of each (Figure 7). Carefully cut out each joint and, after a dry-fit, glue the four corners of the box together at 90 degree angles.

10. When the box is finished, measure 1¹/₂" down from the top of each leg to locate the position of the top of the box. Using a fine handsaw and sharp chisel, cut a ¹/₂" wide by ¹/₈" deep dado on the two adjacent sides (Figure 8) of each leg. Fit this two-sided notch be-

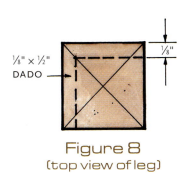

¹/₈" × ¹/₂" DADO

¹/₈"

Figure 8
(top view of leg)

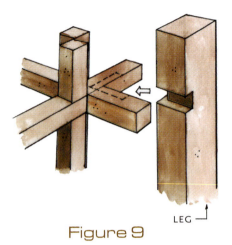

Figure 9

LEG

tween the two crossed arms at the top of one corner of the box as shown in Figure 9. Mark the position of the crossed arms at the bottom of the box empirically and cut another pair of $1/8$" deep dadoes in the leg piece. Repeat for each leg. Be sure to make an identifying mark at each corner of the box and on each leg so you can match up the notches when it comes time to fit them together.

11. Clamp all four legs in position using two strap-clamps (without glue in the joints) and set the lamp upright. The bottoms of the legs must sit flat on a level surface to keep the lamp perfectly vertical. Check this with a builder's level (Figure 10). Adjust the notches if necessary and when all is level and square, sand each leg. Put glue in the dadoes and re-clamp the assembly.

12. Drill a $3/8$" diameter hole $5/8$" deep, centered in the top of each leg (Figure 11). Use dowel centers to locate the corresponding holes in the underside of the top, which

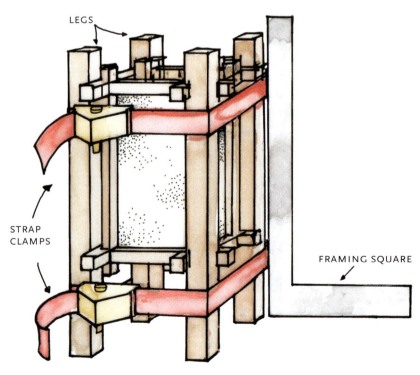

LEGS

STRAP CLAMPS

FRAMING SQUARE

Figure 10

will be attached to the legs with four ³/₈" diameter dowels, 1" long. Note: Each of these dowels will be centered on the 45 degree joint in the top.

13. Drill the four ⁵/₈" deep holes in the top then, using a standard handplane, shape the curved upper edges of the top by eye. A long gentle curve is more appropriate here than a simple rounded corner. It is more work, but worth the effort.

14. Sand the top. Glue the four dowels in place with the top of the lamp attached to the legs, then let the assembly dry while standing upright with a weight on top.

15. Finish the top and legs with at least two coats of wax, oil, or clear varnish.

16. Screw a one-by-three, 6" long, to the underside of the box frame as shown in the top view and side view. This piece, centered on two sides of the box, should have a ³/₈" diameter hole drilled through the center (Figure 12) to attach a standard, threaded light socket nipple.

17. Screw a 1¹/₄" long nipple into the ³/₈" diameter hole so it threads itself into the wood. Let the nipple protrude below the wooden bar enough to allow a lockwasher and nut. Pass an 18 ga. electrical cord up through the hole in the nipple and through the bottom half of a standard light socket. Divide the wires and tie a knot in them as shown in Figure 13. Attach the wires to the light socket, assemble the socket, and screw it onto the nipple. Attach a switch to the cord about one foot away from the lamp and attach a plug to the end of the cord (see the Appendix on page 122).

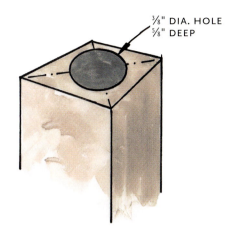

³/₈" DIA. HOLE
⁵/₈" DEEP

Figure 11

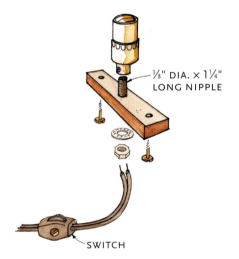

³/₈" DIA. × 1¹/₄"
LONG NIPPLE

SWITCH

Figure 12

Figure 13

CRYPTOMERIA
(SUGI)
TEMPLE LANTERN

This charming lantern, patterned after those used for centuries in Japanese temples, is another one originally designed for a candle or perhaps a dish of oil. The rectangular box frame is topped by a gracefully curved roof which is, in turn, reminiscent of those of ancient buildings. The curved exterior ribs and the small mullions provide much interesting detail, making this lantern an attractive accent whether it is lighted or not.

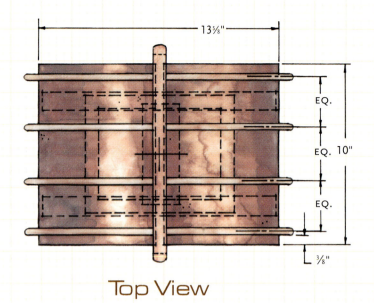

Top View

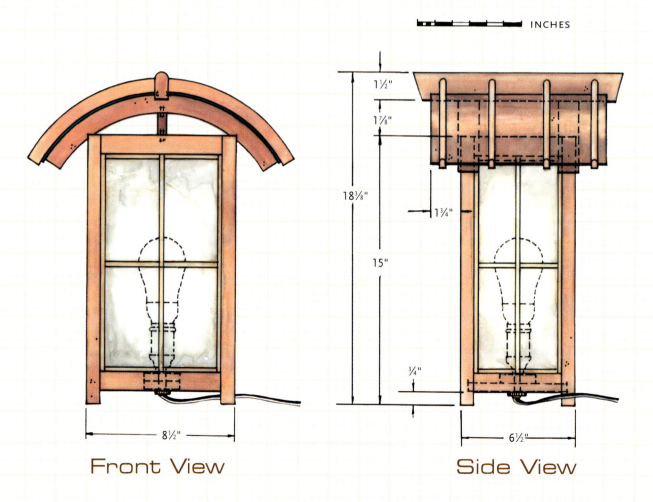

Front View

Side View

INCHES

Method

1. From ³/₄" square hardwood (cherry, walnut, maple, ash, etc.) cut four corner posts each 15" long.

2. From ³/₄" × 1" hardwood cut four horizontal pieces 7" long each and four 5" long each. Two of each of the 7" and 5" pieces will be used at the top of the frame and two at the bottom. Drill a ³/₈" hole ¹/₄" deep centered in the ends of all eight pieces.

3. Centered in the lower inside edge of two of the 7" long bottom horizontal pieces only, cut a recess ¹/₂" × ¹/₂" × 2" as shown in Figure 1. These will be used to mount the socket base (step 10).

4. With ³/₈" diameter dowel centers in the ends of one of the top horizontals, line it up flush with the ends of two of the corner posts as shown in Figure 2. Press the posts together to mark the centers for dowel holes then repeat with the other three top horizontals.

5. Repeat step 4 with the bottom horizontals except place them ³/₄" up from the bottom ends of the corner posts (see front and side views).

6. Drill ³/₈" diameter holes ¹/₄" deep at every location marked by the dowel centers on the corner posts. Cut sixteen ¹/₂" lengths of ³/₈" diameter doweling.

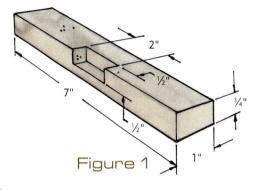

Figure 1

Figure 2

Tools

- Tablesaw and bandsaw
- Drill with ⅛", ⅜", and ¾" drill bits
- Handplane
- Chisel – ⅛" wide
- Wood rasp
- Two barclamps and two or more spring clamps
- Dowel-centering points
- Marking gauge
- Bench square
- Utility knife and/or scissors

Materials

- Corner posts – four pieces of ¾" square hardwood 15" long
- Horizontals – front and back: four pieces of hardwood ½" × 1" × 7" each. Sides: four pieces of hardwood ½" × 1" × 5" each.
- Mullions – twelve verticals ³⁄₁₆" square × 12" long each. Twelve horizontals ³⁄₁₆" × 5" long each.
- Roof beams – cut from two pieces of ¾" hardwood 4" × 13 ½" each
- Roof beam supports – two pieces ⁵⁄₁₆" square × 1 ⅜" each
- Roof ribs – cut from eight pieces of ⅜" hardwood 1¾" × 8½" each
- Ridge beam – ¾" hardwood 1½" × 12"
- Roof – two pieces of ⅛" softwood 7¾" × 10" each
- Base – ½" plywood 2" × 6"
- Lamp socket mounting block – ½" plywood 2" square
- Shoji – two sheets of mulberry paper 7" × 12" each and two sheets 5" × 12"
- Carpenter's glue – white or yellow
- Standard electric lamp socket with a 1½" long threaded nipple (⅜" diameter), six feet of 18 ga. lamp cord with a switch and plug

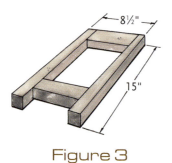

Figure 3

7. Glue a dowel into both ends of a top and a bottom horizontal (both of them 7" long) and, with glue on the end of the dowels, clamp them in place to form a front frame (Figure 3). Repeat this to make up a back frame. After the glue has dried, glue and clamp both sides' top and bottom horizontals (all of them 5" long) together with dowels, to form the rectangular box as shown in the front and side views.

8. Trim lengths of 3/16" square fir mullion strips to fit vertically and horizontally inside each of the framed panels arranged as shown in the front and side views. Glue and clamp them flush with the inside edges of the openings (Figure 4).

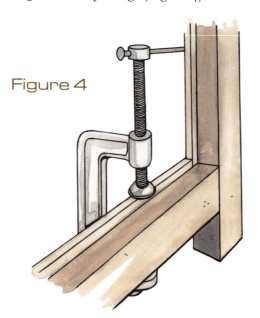

Figure 4

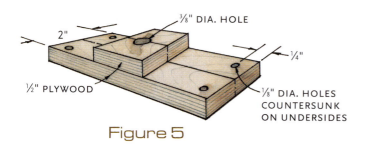

Figure 5

9. From 1/2" plywood, cut out a 2" × 6" base and a socket mounting block 2" square. Find the centers of both pieces and drill a 3/8" diameter hole in each. Line up the holes over each other and glue the two blocks together. Drill two 1/8" holes 1/4" in from each end of the base (Figure 5) and countersink the underside of each.

10. Screw a 1 1/2" long threaded nipple to the lower half of a standard lamp socket then screw it through the center hole in the mounting block/base assembly. Fasten a nut and washer to the underside. Lead one end of the 18 ga. lamp cord up through the nipple, separate the wires for about 3", and tie a reefknot in them. Attach the ends of the wires to the lamp socket proper, slip the cardboard tube and the brass sleeve over it, then snap the assembly in place on the lower half of the socket. Attach a plug to the end of the cord and a switch about one foot away from the base.

11. Using the pattern (Figure 6), enlarged on a photocopier, bandsaw two roof beams from 3/4" thick hardwood 4" × 13 1/2". Note: The lower notches shown on the pattern should be exactly the width of the front of the rectangular box. They are used to register their position. Drill 1/8" diameter holes 1/4" deep centered on (but 5/32" from the back edge of) the underside of both of the roof beams. Do the same on the tops of the front and back faces of the box (see Figure 7).

12. Cut two pieces of 5/16" square fir to fit between the top of the box and the underside of the roof beams. Drill 1/8" diameter holes in the ends of the two roof beam supports and glue 1/8" dowels (3/8" long) into them.

13. Glue the roof beams in place on top of the box, with the supports between them and all flush with the inside edge as shown in Figure 8.

14. From 3/4" hardwood, make a ridge beam 1 1/2" × 12" long. Cut the ends at a 15 degree angle (see side view) and round the

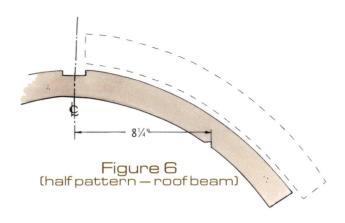

8 1/4"

Figure 6
(half pattern — roof beam)

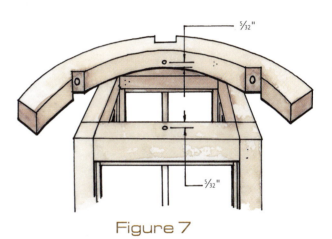

5/32"

5/32"

Figure 7

5/16" SQUARE FIR

Figure 8

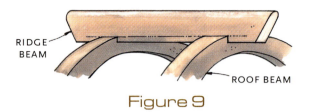

Figure 9

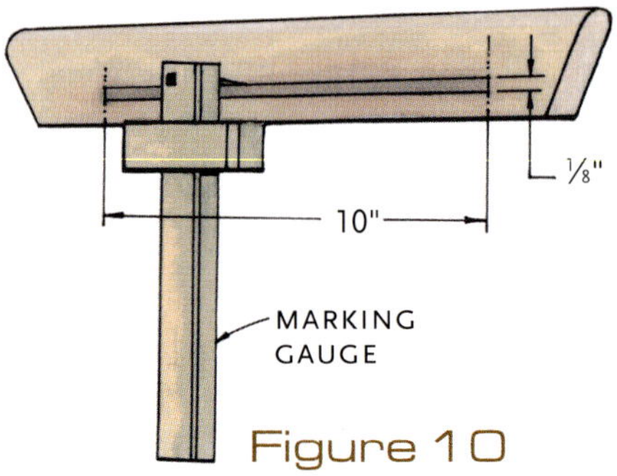

Figure 10

Figure 11

top edge nicely with a handplane and sandpaper. Fit the ridge beam snugly into the notches in the roof beams and mark the exact position of the tops of the roof beams on either side of the ridge beam (Figure 9). With a marking gauge, scribe a line on either side of the ridge beam to match these marks (Figure 10). Extend the marking gauge $1/8$" and scribe marks parallel to the first ones. Using a $1/8$" wide chisel and the scribed lines as a guide (Figure 11), cut $3/16$" deep slots only 10" long (centered along the length of the ridge beam) on both sides. The roof panels will be inserted into these slots. Glue the ridge beam in place on the roof beams.

15. From $1/8$" fir, cut out two roof panels $7^3/4$" × 10" with the grain following the 10" dimension to facilitate bending (see Figure 12). With glue along one 10" edge and on the top of the roof beams, insert one of the roof panels into the slot in the ridge beam and clamp it to the roof

Figure 12

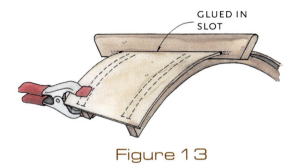

Figure 13

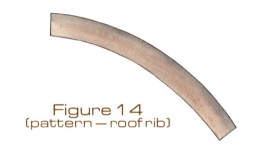

Figure 14
(pattern — roof rib)

beams with spring clamps (Figure 13). Repeat with the other roof panel.

16. Using the pattern (Figure 14), enlarged on a photocopier, bandsaw eight roof ribs from $3/8$" thick hardwood $1^3/4$" × $8^1/2$" long. Round the top edges with a handplane and sandpaper.

17. Glue the outer ribs to the roof panels using spring clamps; position them $3/8$" from the edges.

18. Glue the remaining two ribs on each side equidistant from each other between the outer ones.

19. Cut two pieces of shoji (mulberry paper) 7" × 12" and two pieces 5" × 12". Unscrew the base from the box and glue the shoji to the inside faces of the mullions. Spray water on the paper with an atomizer.

20. Screw a tall mini-fluorescent bulb into the lamp socket and fasten the base in place in the recesses cut into the underside of the 7" horizontals (see Figure 1).

21. Finish the wood on the lantern with oil or varnish.

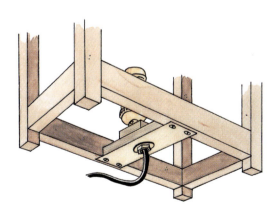

Figure 15

Wisteria (Fuji) Floor Lantern

This lantern is reminiscent of a previous floor lamp, the Morning Glory. A light, papered box glows beneath a rather heavy top, supported by four sturdy legs, gracefully curved at the bottom. This lantern is more than twice the size of the Morning Glory, and is quite suitable as a floor lantern.

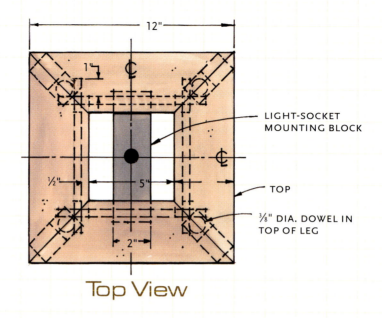

12"

1"

℄

LIGHT-SOCKET
MOUNTING BLOCK

½"　5"

℄

TOP

2"

⅜" DIA. DOWEL IN
TOP OF LEG

Top View

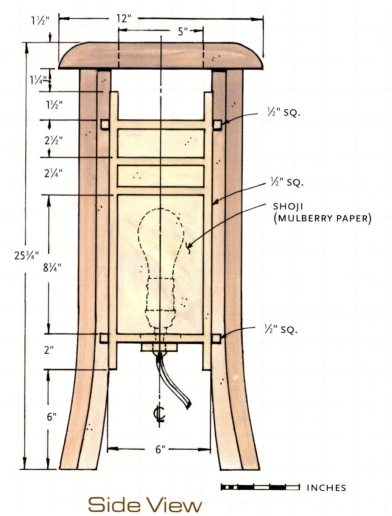

1½"　12"　5"

1¼"

1½"　　½" SQ.

2½"

2¼"　　½" SQ.

SHOJI
(MULBERRY PAPER)

25¾"　8¾"

½" SQ.

2"

℄

6"

6"

INCHES

Side View

Method

1. Use two-by-four stock to make the top of the lamp. Cut four foot-long pieces with carefully sawn 45 degree angles at each end. With a tablesaw, cut 1/2" wide × 1/2" deep slots in the mitred faces which stop before the cut through the outside corners (Figure 1). Make four 1/2" × 1" splines.

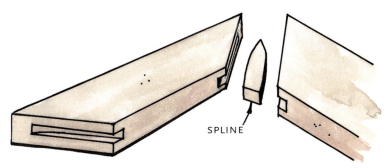

SPLINE

Figure 1

2. With the splines glued in place and glue on the mitred faces, clamp the four sides of the top together simultaneously. There are several methods for clamping as shown in Figure 2: Method A – two bar- or pipe-clamps

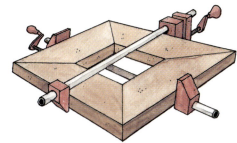

Figure 2
Method A

Tools
- Tablesaw, bandsaw, and small crosscut, handsaw
- Drill with 1/4", 3/8", and 1/2" diameter bits
- Handplane
- Chisel – 1/2" wide
- Utility knife
- Builder's square
- A strap-clamp, bar-clamp, or picture frame clamp
- Screwdriver
- Dowel-centering points
- Bench square
- Atomizer

Materials
- Top – two-by-four, 50" long, cut into four equal pieces
- Legs – four cut from a two-by-four, each 22½" long
- Screen frames – twenty-four pieces ½" square each cut from two-by-six hardwood board, 17" long
- Mounting block – ½" × 2" × 8" hardwood
- Wood dowel – ½" diameter × 16" hardwood
- Shoji – mulberry paper 12" × 24" (you could also use one of the handmade papers available at art supply stores)
- Carpenter's glue – white or yellow
- Standard electric light socket with 1" long threaded nipple (3/8" diameter) and six feet of 18 ga. electrical cord with a switch and plug

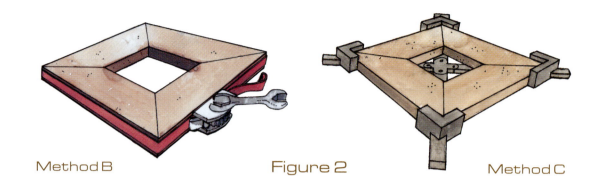

Method B   Figure 2   Method C

Figure 3

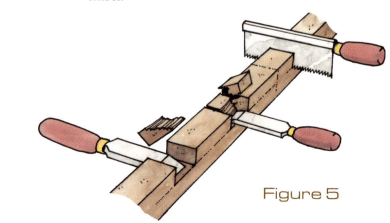

Figure 4

Method B – a single strap-clamp with ratchet tightener
Method C – a commercially available picture frame clamp

3. Cut four pieces 22¹/₂" long for the legs from two-by-four stock. Using a bandsaw or jigsaw, cut out one edge and one corner of each piece (Figure 3) to match the pattern shown on side view (page 66).

4. The "body" of the lamp consists of four papered screens joined to form a square box. Make the screens separately from ¹/₂" square hardwood lap-jointed pieces cut from two-by-six hardwood with paper glued on the back.

5. For each screen cut six ¹/₂" square pieces as shown in Figure 6: two pieces 17" long, two pieces 8" long, and two pieces 6" long. On each piece mark out the location of each ¹/₄" deep notch (see Figure 4) used for lap joints, using a set square. As shown in Figure 5, cut each notch carefully with a fine handsaw and sharp chisel.

Figure 5

6. Press-fit all the lap joints together at once (without glue) as a trial run. Use a chisel to clean up or enlarge any notch showing signs of resistance until the frame lies flat and each corner is at a perfect 90 degrees (Figure 6). Reassemble the frame with a thin layer of glue in each joint and place a piece of plywood over the frame with several weights on top to hold it in place until the glue has dried. Repeat this process with the other three frames.

7. Carefully sand and finish each frame with oil, wax, or varnish, leaving the inside face bare so the paper can be glued to it.

8. Thin some carpenter's glue with water and spread it carefully over the back of each piece of the frame. Lay a sheet of rice paper on the frame, being careful to avoid wrinkles or creases. Once the glue has dried, mist water over both sides of the paper with an atomizer to shrink it. While the paper dries, lay the frame upside down on a flat surface with a weight at each corner (Figure 7).

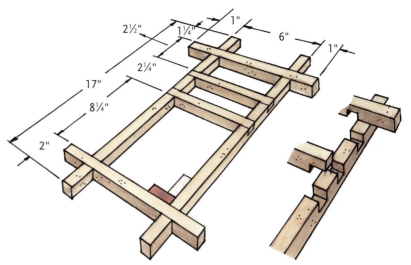

Figure 6

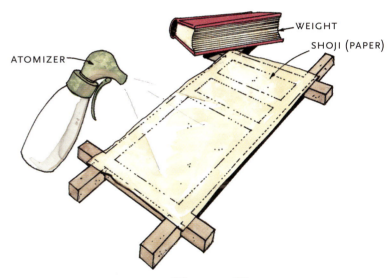

ATOMIZER

WEIGHT

SHOJI (PAPER)

Figure 7

9. Join the four screens together in a square box shape with lap joints in the top and bottom cross pieces of each (Figure 8). Carefully cut out each joint and, after a dry-fit, glue the four corners of the box together at 90 degree angles.

10. The legs should be 45 degree angles to the corners of the lamp with the protruding arms of the box notched into them (Figure 9). Measure 3" down from the top of each leg to locate the upper notches as shown in Figure 10. Cut this notch into each leg then

Figure 8

Figure 9

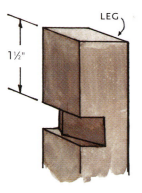

Figure 10

fit each to a corresponding corner of the box (Figure 11). Mark out the exact location of the bottom notch in each leg empirically, then cut each to fit the lower arms of the box. Clamp the legs to the box dry with two strap-clamps and set the lamp upright. The bottoms of the legs must all sit flat on a level surface with the lamp perfectly vertical. Check this with a builder's level (Figure 12).

11. Adjust the notches if necessary and when all is level and square, sand each leg. Put glue in the notches and clamp the four legs to the lamp until dry.

12. Drill a 1/2" diameter hole 5/8" deep, centered in the top of each leg (Figure 13). Using the dowel-centers, locate the corresponding holes in the underside of the top, which will be attached to the legs with four 1/2" diameter dowels, 1" long. Note: Each of these dowels will be centered on the 45 degree joint in the top.

13. Drill the four 5/8" deep holes in the top then use a standard hand-plane to shape the curved upper edges of the top by eye. A long, gentle curve is more appropriate than a simple rounded corner. It is more work but worth the effort. Sand the top. Glue the four dowels in place with the top of the lamp attached to the legs then

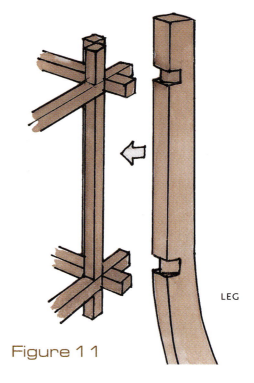

Figure 11

let the assembly dry while standing up-right with a weight on top.

14. Finish the top and legs with at least three coats of oil, wax, or clear varnish.

15. Screw a one-by-three, 6" long to the underside of the box frame as shown in the top and side views. This piece, centered on two sides of the box, should have a ³/₈" diameter hole drilled through the center (Figure 14) to attach a standard, threaded light socket nipple.

16. Screw a 1¹/₄" long nipple into the ³/₈" diameter hole so it threads itself into the wood. Let the nipple protrude below the wooden bar enough to allow a lockwasher and nut. Pass an 18 ga. electrical cord up through the hole in the nipple and through the bottom half of a standard light socket. Divide the wires and tie a knot in them as shown in Figure 15. Attach the wires to the light socket, assemble the socket, and screw it onto the nipple. Attach a switch to the cord about one foot away from the lamp and attach a plug to the end of the cord.

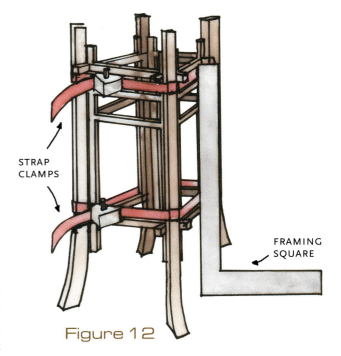

STRAP CLAMPS

FRAMING SQUARE

Figure 12

½" DIA. HOLE
⅝" DEEP

Figure 13

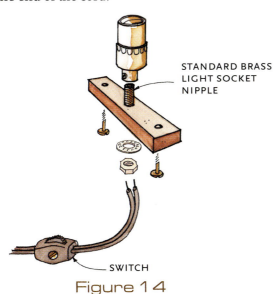

STANDARD BRASS LIGHT SOCKET NIPPLE

SWITCH

Figure 14

Figure 15

Edo Floor
Lantern

This floor lantern is a tall, elegant expression of the Japanese style. With a tall mini-fluorescent bulb inside it is like a softly glowing, four-sided shoji screen. It can be strategically placed on the floor of any room to direct traffic, separate furniture design themes, or define spatial elements. One or more of these lamps can set the tone of even a large room.

The basic, papered box is simply mounted on two curved feet. The paper used in this lantern can be chosen from the wide variety of handmade translucent papers available from most art supply stores. The height of this lantern may make it necessary to apply the paper in several pieces on each side.

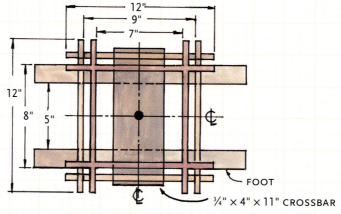

12"
9"
7"
12"
8"
5"
₵
₵
FOOT
¾" × 4" × 11" CROSSBAR

Top View

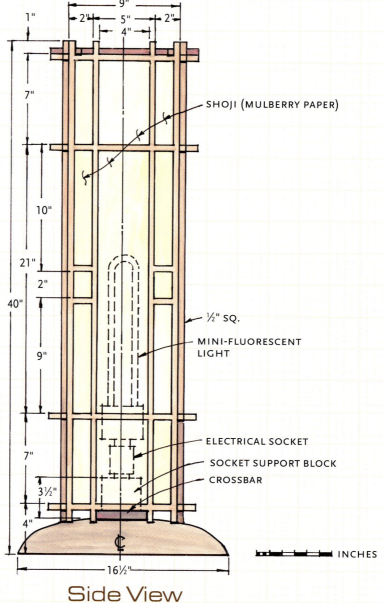

1"
9"
2"
5"
2"
4"
7"
10"
21"
2"
40"
9"
7"
3½"
4"
16½"

SHOJI (MULBERRY PAPER)

½" SQ.

MINI-FLUORESCENT LIGHT

ELECTRICAL SOCKET

SOCKET SUPPORT BLOCK

CROSSBAR

₵

INCHES

Side View
(four sides the same)

Method

1. Study the dimensions of the four-sided screened box as shown in Figure 1. Construct this box by following the directions for Wisteria floor lamp in steps 3 to 7 on pages 68 and 69. The dimensions, as well as the number of pieces, are different but the method is identical.

2. To mute the light at the top of this lantern, construct a frame of four $1/2$" square pieces, each one foot long, with lap joints. Then sand the frame and wax, oil, or varnish and apply matching paper. This cover can rest on top of the lantern without being fastened in place to give easy access to the light fixture inside.

3. The base for this lantern consists simply of two "feet" attached to a crossbar. From $3/4$" × $2^3/4$" hardwood matching that of the box frame, cut two 17" long feet from the pattern below. Sand these pieces ready for finishing.

4. Make the crossbar from $3/4$" thick hardwood 4" wide by 11" long. Drill two pairs of $1/8$" diameter holes at each end: one pair $3/4$" from each end and one pair $1^3/4$" from each end (Figure 1). Center the two feet under the second pair of holes and screw the crossbar to the feet.

5. To raise the light from the very bottom of the lantern, the socket should be mounted on a block of wood attached to the crossbar. Make a hardwood block 3" square by $2^3/4$" high and drill a $3/8$" diameter hole through the center for a socket nipple. Drill a $3/8$" diameter hole in the center of the crossbar for the electrical cord and glue the mounting block over it. Turn a 4" long threaded nipple into the holes in the mounting block and crossbar. Let the nipple protrude below the wooden crossbar enough to allow a lockwasher and nut. Screw the bottom half of a standard brass light socket onto the top of the nipple. Pass an 18 ga. electrical cord up through the hole in the nipple and socket, separate the wires, and tie a knot in them. Attach the wires to the light socket and screw it onto the nipple.

6. Finally, with four 1" long roundhead brass screws, fasten the crossbar to the underside of the box frame as shown in Figure 2. An elongated mini-fluorescent light is ideal in this lantern.

Tools

- Tablesaw, bandsaw, and small crosscut handsaw
- Drill with $1/4$" and $3/8$" diameter bits
- Chisel – $1/2$" wide
- Utility knife and/or scissors
- Screwdriver
- Builder's level
- Atomizer

Materials

- Feet – two cut from a hardwood two-by-four, 17" long
- Crossbar – $3/4$" × 4" × 11" hardwood
- Mounting block – 3" × 3" × $2^1/2$" hardwood
- Four screen frames – twelve $1/2$" square pieces for each frame cut from a hardwood two-by-ten, 38" long
- Rice paper (or other decorative paper, preferably translucent) – four sheets 9" × 36" and one sheet 9" square
- Six brass roundhead screws – $1^1/2$" long
- Four brass roundhead screws – 1" long
- Electric light socket and six feet of electrical wire with a switch attached and a plug
- Carpenter's glue – white or yellow

Autumn Moon (Tsuki) Wall Light

I am not aware of interior wall lamps being used in Japan until modern times but this has a very traditional look. It is simply a deep octagonal box frame covered with rice paper. Mounted on a wall over a one- or two-bulb fixture, the Autumn Moon light will glow softly like its namesake.

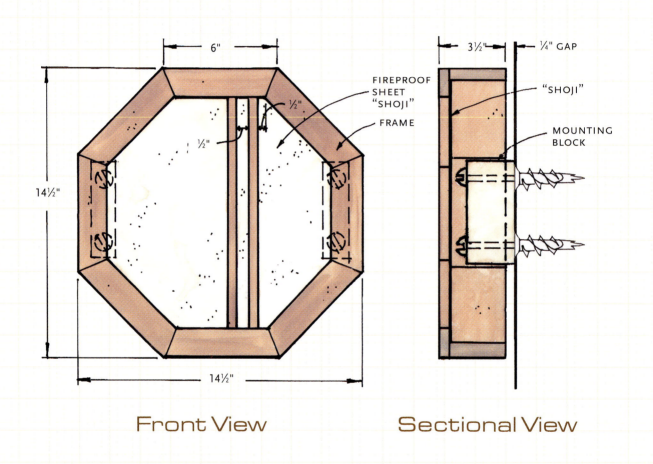

6"

½"

½"

FIREPROOF
SHEET
"SHOJI"

FRAME

14½"

14½"

3½"

¼" GAP

"SHOJI"

MOUNTING
BLOCK

Front View

Sectional View

INCHES

Method

1. Using western red cedar or an interesting hardwood, cut eight pieces $1^1/2$" × $3^1/2$" × 6" long to make the sides of the frame. Cut a 1" × $3^1/8$" rabbet lengthwise in these pieces on a tablesaw as shown in Figure 1.

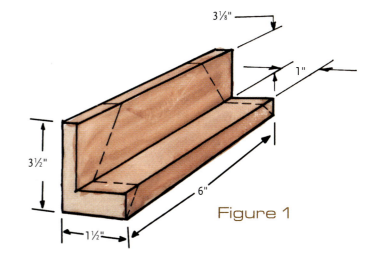

3⅛"

1"

3½"

6"

1½"

Figure 1

2. Mark $22^1/2$ degree angles at either end of the eight pieces on the $1^1/2$" wide face using an adjustable square (Figure 2). Using a handsaw or tablesaw, cut the angled ends ready to clamp together.

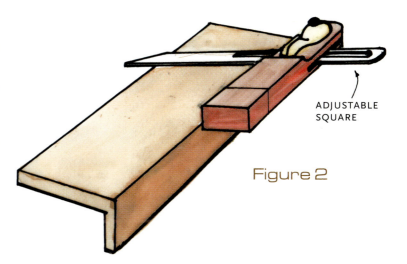

ADJUSTABLE SQUARE

Figure 2

Tools
- Tablesaw and small crosscut handsaw
- Adjustable square
- Two strap-clamps
- Chisel – ½" wide
- Atomizer
- Utility knife and/or scissors
- Drill with a ⅛" diameter bit
- Screwdriver

Materials
- A softwood such as western red cedar works well for this lamp, as do various hardwoods, such as maple, cherry, or walnut
- Sides – eight 6" long sides with mitered corners cut from two-by-fours, 48" long
- Center strips – two wooden strips ⅜" × ½" × 13" long each
- Mounting blocks – two wood blocks 1½" × 2" × 5" long each

- Fireproof paper sheet 12" square, (you can substitute other handmade decorative papers, available at art supply stores)
- Four roundhead screws
- Wall-mounted single or double bulb light fixture
- Sandpaper – 220 and 120 grit
- Carpenter's glue – white or yellow

3. Using two ratchet-type strap-clamps as shown in Figure 3, clamp all eight sides at once in a dry run. If the angles have been cut accurately and perfectly perpendicular to the back of the frame, the assembly will be symmetrical. Glue and re-clamp the frame and let it dry.

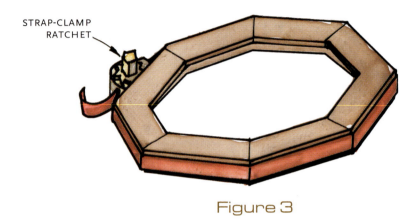

STRAP-CLAMP
RATCHET

Figure 3

4. Cut two pieces of wood, matching that of the frame, $3/8$" × $1/2$" and at least 13" long. These decorative strips of wood will provide support for the rice paper. Bevel the ends of these pieces to fit in matching beveled mortises in the frame as shown in Figure 4. Cut the mortises with a small saw and chisel. Trim the two pieces to their exact length while fitting them to the frame. Once this is done, glue them in place. The frame can now be sanded and fin-

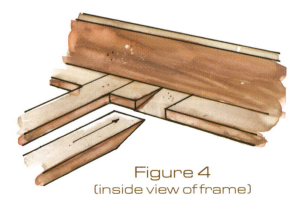

Figure 4
(inside view of frame)

ished with wax, oil, or several coats of clear varnish. Do not get any finishing material on the inside face of the frame.

5. Keeping the frame face down, fit a piece of fire-proof paper to the inside. To do this, lay the sheet of paper over the frame and carefully rub a pencil

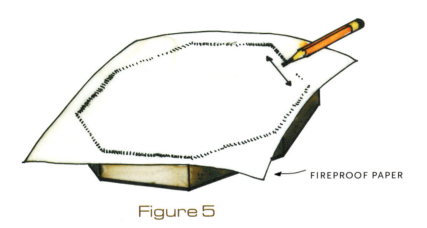

FIREPROOF PAPER

Figure 5

over it where it crosses the inside edge of the frame (Figure 5). This edge will show up as a pattern of the inside. Cut this out with scissors.

6. Put a thin coat of glue on the inside face of the frame and two decorative strips and then press the paper in place. With an atomizer, mist water on the paper to shrink it tight.

7. Make two wooden mounting blocks $1^1/2" \times 2" \times 5"$ that can be screwed to the wall on either side of a commercially available wall-mounted light socket (Figure 6). Using the frame itself as a guide, position the blocks so the wooden octagon can be press-fit into place.

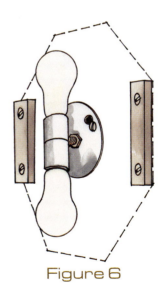

Figure 6

Plum Blossom (Ume) Wall Light

This curved wall sconce is made up of a very lightweight frame lined with rice paper. The curved pieces are laminated over a semi-circular form similar to the method described for the Cherry Blossom table lantern on page 9. The rings on the table lantern are complete circles, but the technique is identical for this light.

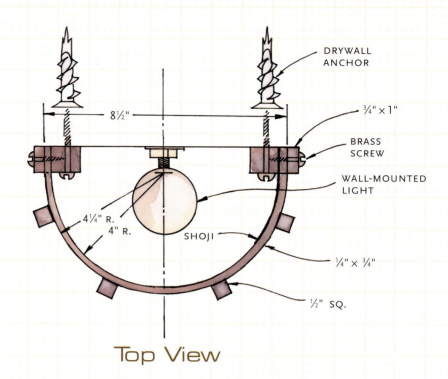

DRYWALL
ANCHOR

¾" × 1"

BRASS
SCREW

WALL-MOUNTED
LIGHT

8½"

4¼" R.
4" R.

SHOJI

¼" × ¾"

½" SQ.

Top View

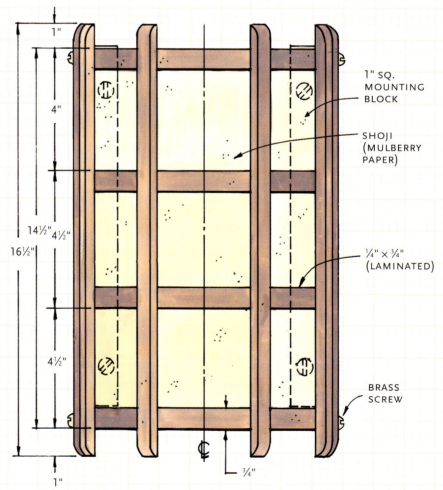

1"

4"

14½"

4½"

16½"

4½"

1"

¾"

1" SQ.
MOUNTING
BLOCK

SHOJI
(MULBERRY
PAPER)

¼" × ¾"
(LAMINATED)

BRASS
SCREW

INCHES

Front View

Method

1. Cut two 16½" lengths of ¾" × 1" hardwood. Cut four ¼" deep notches in the back face of both pieces as shown in Figure 1. Cut four 16½" lengths of ½" square hardwood to match. Using a saw, chisel, and sandpaper, shape the ends of all six pieces into a curved bevel as shown in Figure 2. Sand all pieces.

2. Using the top view on page 86 as a guide, cut out two semi-circular pieces of ¾" plywood to make the ends of a form (Figure 3). The shape is actually more than an exact semi-circle; an extra 1" is added to a 8½" diameter semi-circle along the flat side.

Figure 1

Figure 2
(detail)

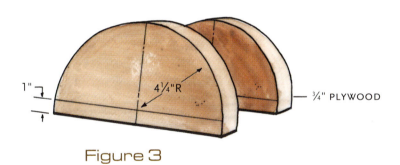

1"

4¼"R

¾" PLYWOOD

Figure 3

Tools
- Tablesaw and small crosscut handsaw
- Drill with ⅛" diameter bit
- Chisel – ½" wide
- Atomizer
- Utility knife and/or scissors
- Two bar-clamps
- Screwdriver

Materials
- Vertical bars – six made of hardwood, two: ¾" square × 16½" long each, and four: ½" square × 16½" long each
- Mounting blocks – two pieces of 1" square hardwood, 10" long each
- Edgebanding – sixteen hardwood ¾" side strips, 16" long
- Forms – three pieces of ¾" plywood 6" × 9" each
- Cardstock or cardboard – 12" × 13"
- Rice paper – 12½" × 15" (you can substitute handmade paper, available from art supply stores)
- Six brass roundhead screws – 1¼" long
- Carpenter's glue – white or yellow
- Wall-mounted single or double bulb light fixture

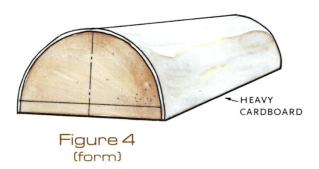

Figure 4
(form)

HEAVY
CARDBOARD

3. Glue a 12$^1/_2$" × 13" piece of heavy cardboard over the plywood forms as shown in Figure 4.

4. Cut out another form with a 4$^1/_4$" radius from $^3/_4$" plywood. Using $^3/_4$" wide strips of hardwood edgebanding and a clothes iron, laminate one layer over another until you have four semi-circles $^1/_4$" thick (Figure 5). Fasten these over the cardboard form spaced as shown in Figure 6 with masking tape at the ends.

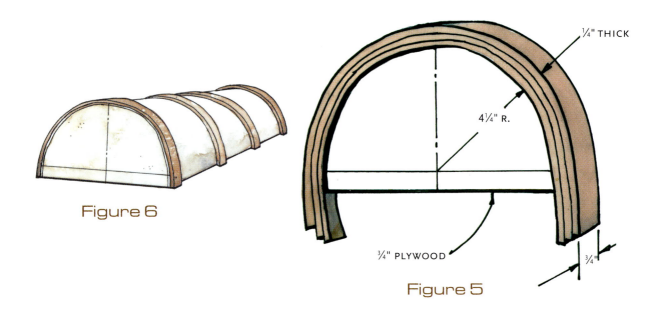

Figure 6

$^1/_4$" THICK

4$^1/_4$" R.

$^3/_4$" PLYWOOD

$^3/_4$"

Figure 5

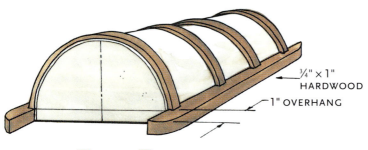

Figure 7

$^3/_4$" × 1"
HARDWOOD

1" OVERHANG

5. Glue and clamp a $^3/_4$" × 1" strip of hardwood to the four semicircles on either side of the form. There will be a 1" overhang at each end. The beveled ends should face outward (Figure 7).

6. Mark the positions for four ¹/₂" square hardwood strips and glue them in place on the curved pieces (Figure 8). When the glue has dried, carefully remove the wood from the form. Do any final sanding and finish with wax, oil, or several coats of clear varnish. Do not apply a finish to the inside face where the paper will be glued in place.

7. Lay rice paper over the form. Dilute a small amount of glue with water and brush it over the inside of the wood frame. Press the frame over the rice paper and clamp it in place on the form until the glue dries. Be very careful to avoid wrinkles. Using an atomizer, mist water on the paper to shrink it tight.

8. Cut two 10" lengths of 1" square hardwood for mounting blocks and drill a ¹/₈" diameter hole ³/₄" from each end. Clamp these flush with the back edge inside the lamp and drill four pilot holes each side as shown in Figure 9. Then screw the two mounting blocks in place on the wall with four drywall anchors on either side of a wall-mounted light fixture (Figure 10). The lamp can now be screwed to the mounting blocks with eight 1¹/₄" long roundhead brass screws.

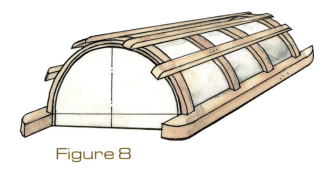

Figure 8

Figure 9

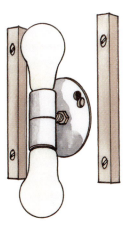

Figure 10

Bellflower (Kikyo) Hanging Lantern

This lantern, like the Peony table lantern, is tall, slim, and round, with wooden hoops and a Lexan® lens. Here the similarities end: the top cap, which is similar to that of the Cherry Blossom, provides a mount for the light socket and the assembly is suspended by a wooden frame. One of the long mini-fluorescent bulbs readily available would be ideal for this handsome lantern.

89

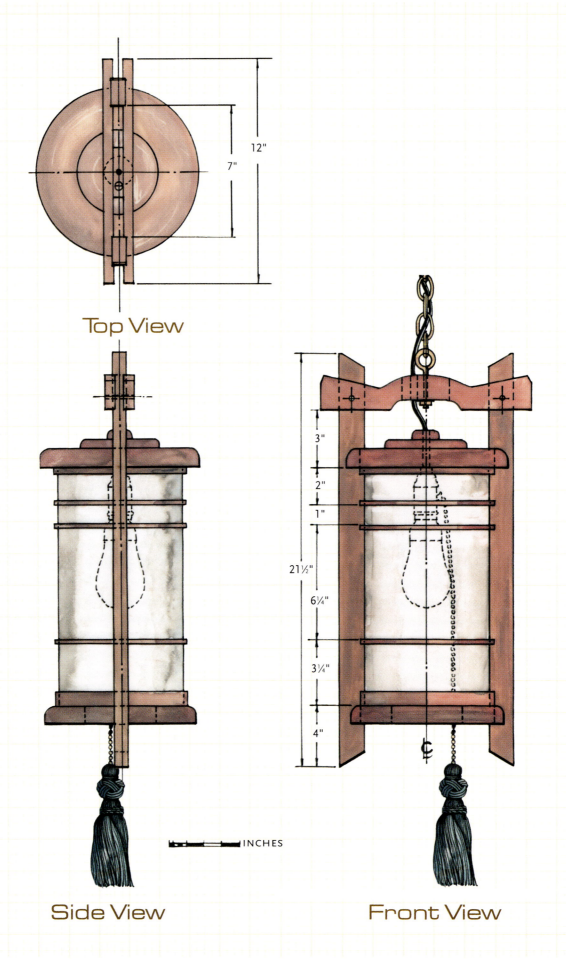

Top View

12"

7"

3"

2"

1"

21½"

6¼"

3¼"

4"

INCHES

Side View

Front View

Method

1. From ³/₄" thick hardwood (cherry, walnut, maple, etc.) cut two verticals 1¹/₄" × 21¹/₂" long each. Cut the bottom ends at 45 degrees and the top ends at 20 degrees. As shown in the side view, the inside edges of the verticals have a series of notches to receive various elements of the lantern. All of them are ¹/₄" deep but they vary in width. To lay out these notches, lay the verticals down with their inside edges facing up and measuring from the bottom angle (1¹/₄" from the end), mark the positions of the base, rings, and top with a bench square to the dimensions shown in Figure 1. Cut these notches with a small handsaw and clean them out with a chisel.

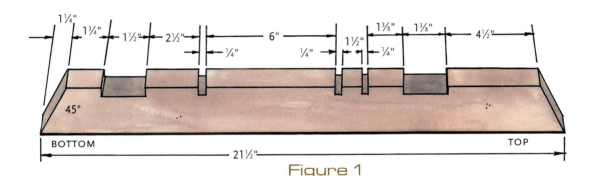

Figure 1

Tools

- Tablesaw, bandsaw, and small crosscut handsaw
- Drill with ¼", ⅜", and ½" bits
- Handplane
- Chisel – ¼" wide
- Bench square
- Wood rasp
- Two bar-clamps and one or more spring clamps
- Drawing compass
- Utility knife and/or scissors
- Clothes iron

Materials:

- Verticals – two from ¾" hardwood 1¼" × 21½" long each
- Crossbars – two from ½" hardwood 1¾" × 12" long each
- Base – 1" hardwood 8½" diameter
- Top – 1" hardwood 9" diameter
- Top cap – ½" hardwood 4½" diameter
- Knobble – ½" hardwood 1½" diameter
- Hardwood edgebanding – ¾" by 12 feet
- Lexan® sheet – 12¾" by 20"

- Carpenter's glue – white or yellow
- Standard electric lamp socket with a pull-chain switch (built in), a 2¼" long threaded nipple (⅜" diameter), and 18 ga. lamp cord (length determined by type of electrical installation)
- Eyebolt – 3" long brass or steel with two nuts and two washers
- Eyebolt mounting block – ½" hardwood 1¼" × 3"
- Chain – brass or steel for hanging lantern (length determined by situation)

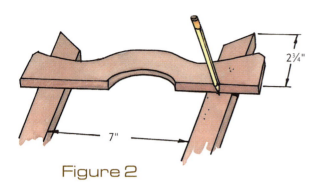

Figure 2

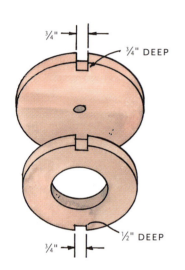

Figure 3

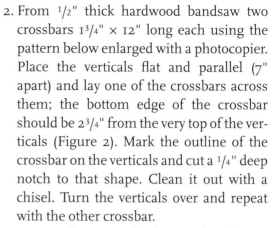

2. From 1/2" thick hardwood bandsaw two crossbars 1 3/4" × 12" long each using the pattern below enlarged with a photocopier. Place the verticals flat and parallel (7" apart) and lay one of the crossbars across them; the bottom edge of the crossbar should be 2 3/4" from the very top of the verticals (Figure 2). Mark the outline of the crossbar on the verticals and cut a 1/4" deep notch to that shape. Clean it out with a chisel. Turn the verticals over and repeat with the other crossbar.

3. With a drawing compass, scribe two circles 8 1/2" and 9" diameter on 1" thick hardwood. The smaller circle will be the base of the lantern and it will require a 4" diameter hole in the center to facilitate changing the light bulb. Bandsaw the two discs and cut the smaller one in half to bandsaw the inside circle. Glue it together again once this has been done. Round the top edges of both discs with a wood rasp and sandpaper as shown in the side view. At either end of the glued joint saw out a 3/4" by 1/2" deep notch in the bottom disc as shown in Figure 3. The top disc requires two similar notches 3/4" wide by 3/4" deep.

4. Make a 4 1/2" diameter top block and a 1 1/2" diameter knobble each from 1/2" thick hardwood, round the top edges, center them over the top, and glue them in place. Drill eight 1/2" diameter holes in the top evenly spaced around the top block to eliminate heat build-up inside the lantern. Finally, drill a 3/8" diameter hole through the center of the knobble, through the top (Figure 4).

5. Screw a 2 1/4" long threaded nipple (3/8" diameter) to the lower half of a standard lamp socket with a built-in pull-chain switch, then screw it through the center hole in the top from the underside. Lead one end of the 18 ga. lamp cord down through the nipple, separate the wires for about 3", and tie a reefknot in it. Attach the ends of the wires to the lamp socket proper, slip the cardboard tube and the brass sleeve over it, then snap the assembly in place on the lower half of the socket (Figure 5).

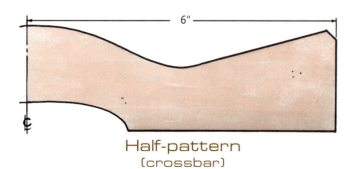

Half-pattern
(crossbar)

6. From ¹/₂" hardwood, make an eyebolt mounting block 1¹/₄" × 3". Drill a ¹/₄" diameter hole through the center of the 3" long edge as shown in Figure 6. Glue this block centered on the inside face of one of the crossbars. Fit the top and bottom discs in their appropriate notches in the verticals and glue and clamp them in place. Glue and clamp the two crossbars in place on either side of the verticals, being sure to glue the eyebolt mounting block to the second crossbar as well. When the assembly has dried, install a 3" eyebolt in the mounting block with a nut and washer above and below as shown in the side view.

7. By the method described on pages 12 and 13 of the first project and using hardwood edgebanding, make five wooden rings: two ¹/₂" wide rings (one for the top and one for the bottom, as shown in the side view) and three ¹/₄" wide rings. All of the rings must have an inside diameter of 7" and they must be no more than ¹/₄" thick. Glue all of the rings in place in their appropriate notches between the verticals being sure that they are concentric.

8. Cut out a sheet of Lexan® 12³/₄" by approximately 20" long, roll it up, and insert it up through the bottom hole, letting it expand inside the rings with the ends forming a butt joint opposite one of the verticals. It is not necessary to glue this in place. (Note: To ensure a perfect fit of the Lexan®, use a method of trial and error with a sheet of stiff paper and use it as a pattern.)

9. Finish the wood on the lantern with oil or varnish.

10. Attach a brass or steel chain to the eyebolt to suspend the lantern in the required location.

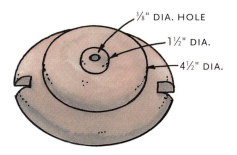

³/₈" DIA. HOLE
1¹/₂" DIA.
4¹/₂" DIA.

Figure 4
(top)

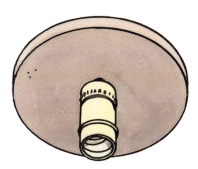

Figure 5

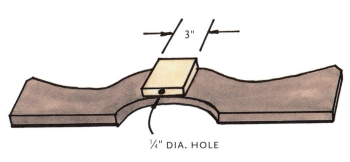

3"

¹/₄" DIA. HOLE

Figure 6

Basho Tree · Hanging Lantern

This lantern, named for Matsuo Basho, the great haiku poet, is the quintessential Japanese lantern. Perhaps because of the traditional Japanese shapes and fine joinery details, it is an image that immediately comes to mind at the mention of Japan and lanterns. Although the lantern is suspended from the ceiling, it is similar to the others in that the light source is a wood-framed papered box.

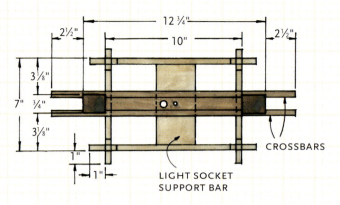

12 ¾"

2½" 10" 2½"

3 ⅛"

7" ¾"

3 ⅛"

1"

1"

CROSSBARS

LIGHT SOCKET
SUPPORT BAR

Top View

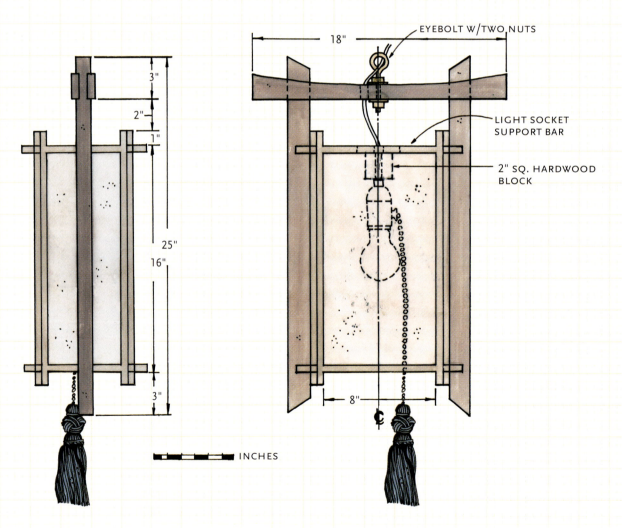

EYEBOLT W/TWO NUTS

18"

LIGHT SOCKET
SUPPORT BAR

2" SQ. HARDWOOD
BLOCK

3"

2"

1"

25"

16"

3"

8"

INCHES

Side View

Front View

Method

1. Study the dimensions of the papered box as shown in Top, Side, and Front views. The box or "body" of the lantern is similar to that of the Morning Glory, Wisteria, and Edo lanterns. See materials list and follow the directions referred to in steps 4 to 9 on pages 68 to 69. The only difference is in the dimensions and the number of horizontal bars of each opposite papered screen.

2. Make two side bars out of 1" × 1¹/₂" hardwood, 25" long each. Cut 1" angles at each end then sand them ready for finishing.

3. Make two crossbars, each 11" long from ¹/₂" × 2" hardwood and then cut out the curved shape shown in the front view on the upper edge of each piece. Sand them ready for finishing.

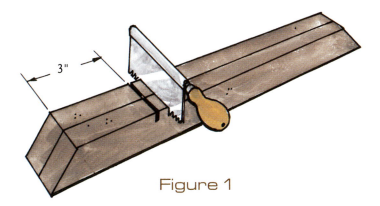

3"

Figure 1

Tools

- Tablesaw, bandsaw, or jigsaw and a small crosscut handsaw
- Drill with ¼" and ⅜" diameter bits
- Bench square
- Small C-clamps – at least four
- Bar-clamps – at least two
- Chisel – ½" wide
- Utility knife and/or scissors
- Atomizer
- Screwdriver

Materials

- Side bars – two hardwood pieces, 1" × 1½", 25½" long each
- Crossbars – two hardwood pieces, ½" × 2" × 18" long each
- Crossbar insert – ½" × 2" × 6" hardwood
- Socket support bar – ½" × 3" × 6" long piece of hardwood
- Socket mounting block – 2" hardwood cube
- Screen frames – four frames, two made with four ½" square hardwood bars: two bars 18" long, and two 9" long; two frames made with four ½" square hardwood bars: two bars 18" long and two 12" long
- Rice paper (or other decorative paper) – two sheets 6" × 16" and two sheets 9" × 16"
- Brass eyebolt c/w nut and washer
- Standard electric light socket with pull-chain switch, 1" long threaded brass nipple, and electrical wire long enough to reach the desired electricity source
- Carpenter's glue – white or yellow

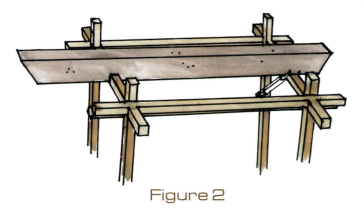

Figure 2

Figure 3

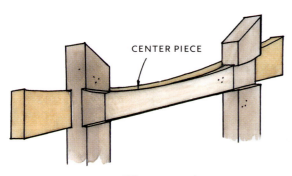

CENTER PIECE

Figure 4

4. Measure 6" down from the top of the inside face of each side bar to locate the top of the papered box frame. Using a bench square and a sharp pencil, mark out a $1/2$" wide by $1/8$" deep dado in each of the side pieces. Carefully cut out these dadoes with a fine saw and a sharp chisel (Figure 1).

5. Fit the dadoes in the side pieces onto the upper bars of the narrow ends of the papered box frame. Mark out the location of the lower bars empirically and saw and chisel dadoes for these out of both side pieces also (Figure 2).

6. Dry-fit and clamp the side pieces onto the box frame (with bar-clamps) centered on the opposing narrow sides. Measure 2" down from the top of the inside face of each of the side pieces to locate the bottom of the two upper crossbars. Lay the bars in this position on either side of the side pieces with a 2" overhang at each end. Mark out a $1/8$" deep dado on either side of each side bar to exactly fit the shape of the crossbars (Figure 3). Cut these dadoes, then glue and clamp the side bars in place on the box frame (see side view).

7. Make a hardwood crossbar insert $3/4$" × $1 1/2$" with a length that matches the distance between the side bars. With glue on the ends, place the insert between the side pieces, keeping the bottom edge flush with the bottom of the dadoes as shown in Figure 4.

8. Glue and clamp the two crossbars in place (in the dadoes) in the side pieces (Figure 5) and to the crossbar insert.

9. Measure and locate the center of the crossbar insert and drill a $1/4$" diameter hole through it to accommodate an eyebolt to suspend the lantern. Beside this hole, drill a second $1/4$" diameter hole through which the electrical cord will pass (see top and front views).

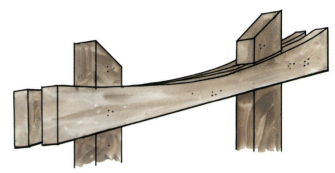

Figure 5

10. Make a hardwood socket support bar $1/2$" × 3" × 6" long and a socket mounting block 3" × 3" × 3". Glue this cube to the center of the support bar and drill a $3/8$" diameter hole through the center of both (Figure 6). Turn a light socket nipple into the hole in the cube.

Figure 6
(light socket support bar)

11. Glue the support bar in place between the upper frame of the papered box. When dry, fasten a wired electrical light socket to the nipple and thread the wire up through the holes in the support bar and the crossbar insert. Attach a plug to the end of the electrical wire if it is to be plugged into a socket. Otherwise have an electrician wire the lantern into the house electrical circuit.

12. Finish the lantern with wax, oil, or at least three coats of varnish.

13. Suspend the lantern from a small brass chain on a hook screwed into the ceiling. The light can be activated from a main room-lighting switch by the entry door or with a pull-chain switch on the socket.

PHOENIX (HOO) HANGING LANTERN

This lantern, one of my favorites, is based on those made by North American designers who worked with oriental themes. In the very early part of the last century it became fashionable on the west coast to suspend large lanterns on leather straps. Many were made with metal but this one is like a tall, tapered wooden box below a small "roof." Perhaps the most chalenging project in the book, the Phoenix lantern is possibly the most spectacular.

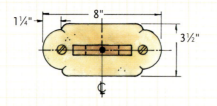

1¼" 8" 3½"

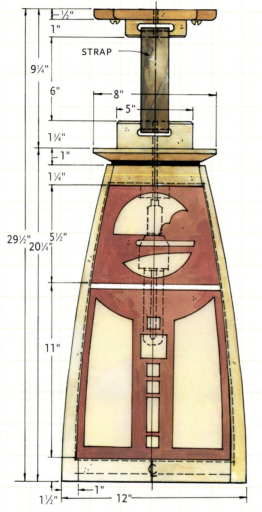

½"
1"
STRAP

9¼"

6" 8"
5"

1¾"
1"
1¼"

29½" 20¼" 5½"

11"

1" 12"
1½"

Front View

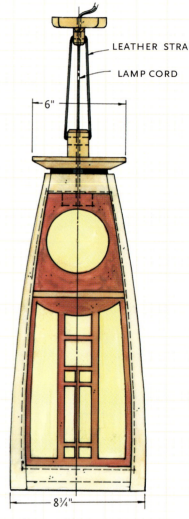

LEATHER STRAP

LAMP CORD

6"

8¾"

Side View

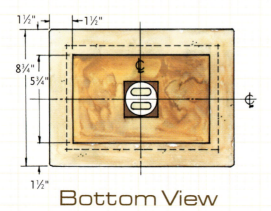

1½" 1½"

8¾"
5¾"

1½"

Bottom View

INCHES

Method

1. Enlarge the three-view drawings opposite on a photocopier to the dimension shown. Cut out four acrylic panels to the size and shape shown, adding $^1/_8$" around the perimeter of each so it can be fit inside the frame. Cut four panels of $^1/_8$" thick maple veneered plywood to match the sizes and shapes of the acrylic panels. Using photocopies as patterns with carbon paper underneath, transfer the designs onto the plywood panels.

2. Cut out the openings in the designs by first drilling a $^1/_4$" diameter hole through the plywood to start the blade of the jigsaw. Sand the edges of the openings with 80 grit sandpaper, then sand each panel with 120 and 220 grit sandpaper, ready for finishing.

3. To make the frame of the lamp, use the full-size three-view drawings as a guide and the curved corner posts as a pattern. Cut four corner posts from four $1^1/_2$" square cherry pieces, each 20" long, on a bandsaw (Figure 1). Cut four upper horizontals from $^1/_2$" × $1^1/_4$" cherry and four lower horizontal pieces from 1" × $1^1/_2$" cherry.

4. Cut a $^1/_4$" square rabbet in the inside corner of each piece as shown in Figure 2. (The lantern, when assembled, will be like

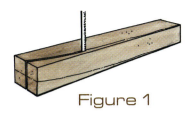

Figure 1

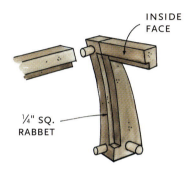

INSIDE FACE

$^1/_4$" SQ. RABBET

Figure 2

Tools

- Tablesaw, bandsaw, and jigsaw
- Drill with $^1/_8$", $^1/_4$", and $^3/_8$" diameter bits and a countersink bit
- Two strap-clamp, and at least four C-clamps
- Chisel – $^3/_8$" wide (or router with $^3/_8$" diameter bit)
- Dowel centering points
- Handplane

Materials

- Frosted acrylic sheets – five pieces, $^1/_{16}$" thick, one: $6^1/_2$" 6 10", two: $10^1/_2$" 6 18", two: $7^1/_4$" 6 18"
- Panels – four pieces of $^1/_8$" maple plywood, two: $10^1/_2$" × 18", two: $7^1/_4$" × 18"
- Corner posts – four cut from

$1^1/_2$" square cherry, each 20" long
- Upper horizontals – four cut from $^1/_2$" × $1^1/_4$" cherry
- Lower horizontals – four cut from 1" × $1^1/_2$" cherry
- Decorative bars – four cut from $^1/_4$" × $^3/_8$" cherry, two: $5^1/_4$" long, two: 8" long
- Top block – $1^1/_2$" cherry, $3^3/_4$" × $5^3/_4$"
- Roof – $^3/_4$" cherry, 6" 6 8"
- Upper strap block – 1" square × 4" long cherry
- Lower strap block – $1^1/_4$" × $1^3/_4$" × 5" cherry
- Ceiling plate – $^1/_2$" cherry $3^1/_2$" × 8"
- Bottom pieces – four cut from $^1/_4$" × $^5/_8$" cherry, two: $5^1/_2$" long, two: $10^1/_8$" long

- Leather strap – $^1/_8$" × 2" × 16"
- Carbon paper – one $8^1/_2$" × 11" sheet
- Drywall anchors – two $1^1/_2$" long
- Screws – four flathead $1^1/_4$" long and four flathead $^1/_2$" long
- Carpenter's glue – white or yellow
- Doweling – $^1/_4$" diameter hardwood, 24" long
- Standard electric light socket with 1" long threaded nipple and a minimum 24" length of electrical wire
- Finish materials – furniture wax, Danish oil, or varnish
- Sandpaper – 80, 120, and 220 grit
- White enamel – 1 spray can

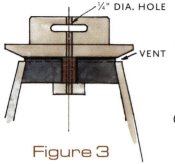

¼" DIA. HOLE

VENT

Figure 3

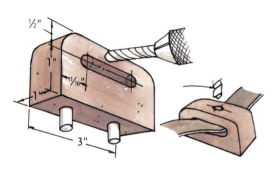

½"

1"

11/16"

1"

3"

Figure 4

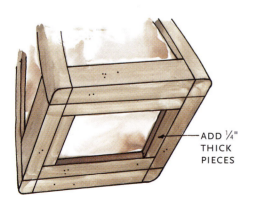

ADD ¼"
THICK
PIECES

Figure 5

four picture frames fastened together in a square.) The rabbet in the eight horizontal pieces can be cut on a tablesaw, but the rabbet in the curved corner posts will have to be cut with a chisel or router.

5. Make doweled corner joints (Figure 2) with dowel centering points and a drill with a ¼" diameter bit. Cut sixteen ¼" diameter dowels ½" long and glue and clamp the whole lantern frame together at once, using strap-clamps.

6. Make the three-piece top assembly as shown in Figure 3, which includes a top block (3¾" × 5¾" × 1½" thick), a roof (6" × 8" × ¾"), and a lower strap block (1¼" × 1¾" × 5"). The top block has 1" × 2" notches cut out of each corner to allow the heat from the light bulb to escape. The roof has 1" × ½" bevels planed around the perimeter on the underside. The lower strap block has a 2¼" wide slot in it, ⅜" deep (Figure 4). To make the slot, drill a ⅜" diameter hole at each end, then cut away a slot in between with a chisel. Glue the top assembly together, then drill a ⅜" diameter hole through the center of it all for the electrical cord. It's a good idea to put two screws into the strap block from the underside of the roof.

7. Turn a threaded nipple into the hole in the underside of the top block and attach a wired electrical socket to it. Run the electrical cord up through the top block and out the side of the slot in the strap block. Fit the top block into the top of the lantern and glue it in place.

8. Glue the plywood panels into the frame and fasten the acrylic panels in behind them with glazing points. To "frost" the sheets of acrylic, spray the inside face with white enamel.

9. Cut out four cherry pieces ¼" × ⅜" as decorative bars: two of them 5¼" long and two of them 8" long. Glue these on the plywood panels as shown in the three-view drawing.

10. Cut out the four cherry bottom pieces ¼" × ⅝": two of them 5½" long and two of them 10⅛" long. Glue these inside the lantern at the bottom as shown in Figure 5. These will form a lip for the fifth acrylic sheet 6½" × 10". Spray the inside face of the acrylic

sheet with white enamel. This sheet will sit loosely in place so the light bulb is accessible.

11. Sand the entire lantern with 120 then 220 grit sandpaper, ready for finishing.

12. Make a ceiling plate from 1/2" thick cherry. This plate is 3 1/2" wide by 8" long. Enlarge the pattern as shown in the three-view drawings and cut out the ceiling plate with a bandsaw.

13. Make an upper strap block from cherry 4" long, 2" wide and 1 1/2" square. Cut a notch out of this block 1/2" deep and 2 1/4" long as shown in Figure 6. Sand this block and the ceiling plate, ready for finishing. Note: These two pieces will be screwed together (with two countersunk flathead screws through the ceiling plate into the strap block) after the leather strap has been attached (Figure 7).

14. Fold a heavy leather strap (2" wide × 16" long) in half and drill a 1/4" diameter hole through it at the fold (the halfway point) (Figure 8). Thread the strap through the slot in the strap block on the lantern, aligning the hole in the strap with the hole in the block. Thread the electrical cord up through these holes.

15. Punch two holes 3/16" away from each end of the strap and fold these ends over each other in the notch in the upper strap block. Screw them in place as shown in Figure 9. Drill a 1/4" diameter hole through both layers of the strap to line up with the hole in the strap block for the electrical cord.

16. Screw the ceiling plate to the upper strap block, threading the electrical cord through the plate. Drill two 1/4" diameter countersunk holes in the ceiling plate for the drywall anchor screws (for mounting on the ceiling) (Figure 10).

17. Finish the lantern and ceiling block with oil, wax, or three coats of varnish. If you use varnish, sand lightly between coats with 220 grit sandpaper. Wax the lantern with furniture wax.

18. Have an electrician connect the electrical wires to a junction box in the ceiling then screw the mounting plate in place with drywall anchors. Note: If the ceiling is made of hard, solid materials, use flathead or roundhead screws.

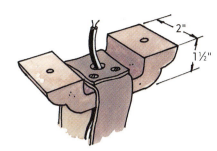

Figure 6

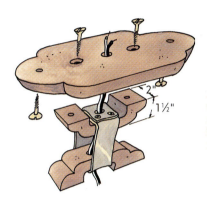

Figure 7

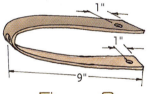

Figure 8

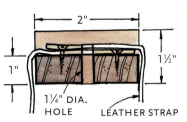

Figure 10

Figure 9

Iris (Kakitsubata) Post Lantern

This outdoor lantern is designed to light a pathway or indicate the entrance to a driveway. The eight vertical slats provide protection for the electric bulb, while the space between the slats will allow light to emerge in an interesting pattern. (The slats, made from Western red cedar, will be durable and can be stained or left to weather gracefully and naturally.)

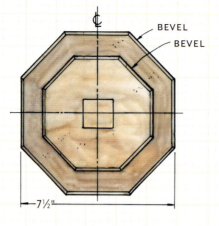

BEVEL
BEVEL

⌀

7½"

Top View

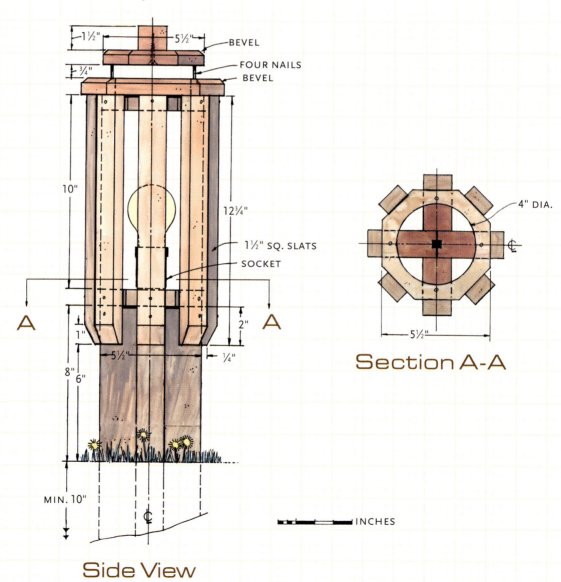

1½"   5½"
BEVEL

FOUR NAILS

¾"

BEVEL

10"

12¾"

1½" SQ. SLATS

SOCKET

A   A

2"

1"

5½"   ¼"

8" 6"

MIN. 10"

⌀

Side View

4" DIA.

⌀

5½"

Section A-A

INCHES

Method

1. Cut two 18" lengths of two-by-three cedar and two 18" lengths of two-by-four. Rip the two-by-fours to a width of $2^1/4$" each, then rip a 1" wide dado along one narrow edge of each of them $1/2$" deep on a tablesaw (Figure 1).

2. Join the four 18" lengths together with water-resistant glue as shown in the top view to form the cruciform post for the lantern, which will be embedded in the ground to about 10". A weatherproof electrical conduit will run from underground up through the 1" square hole in the post to connect to a weatherproof light fixture on the wooden base.

3. From one-by-two cedar stock cut eight vertical slats $12^3/4$". Plane or saw a 1" × $1/2$" bevel at the bottom end of each piece as shown in Figure 2.

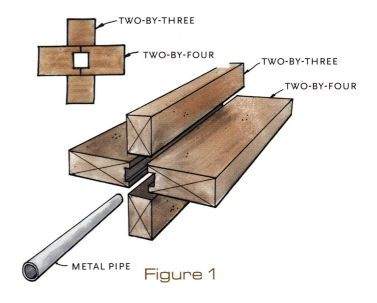

Figure 1

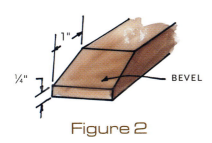

Figure 2

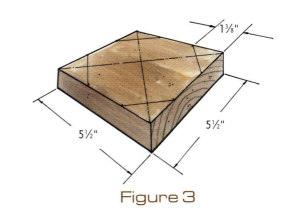

Figure 3

Tools
- Tablesaw, handsaw, and jigsaw
- Drill with $1/8$" and $3/8$" diameter bits
- Hammer
- Bar-clamps – minimum two
- Heavy duty scissors
- Pair of wire cutters

Materials
- Posts – four pieces of red cedar, two: two-by-twos, 18" long each, two: two-by-fours, 18" long
- Slats – eight pieces of one-by-two red cedar, $12^3/4$" long each
- Top – from one-by-eight red cedar, $7^1/2$" long
- Top block – $1^1/2$" red cedar cube
- Base, spacer, and cover – all cut from one-by-six red cedar, $5^1/2$" long each
- Frosted Lexan® or acrylic – $9^1/4$" 6 20", available at plastic supply stores
- Finishing nails – $1^1/2$" galvanized
- All-weather light socket
- Water-resistant glue

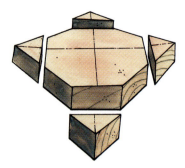

Figure 4

DRILL

Figure 5

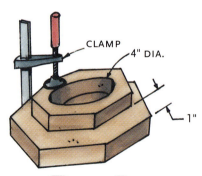

CLAMP

4" DIA.

1"

Figure 6

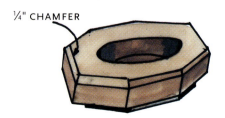

¼" CHAMFER

Figure 7

4. Cut three 5½" lengths from a one-by-six cedar board. Draw corner-to-corner diagonals on one face of each piece to locate the centers. On each of the pieces measure 1⅜" from each corner and connect these points to form an octagon (Figure 3). Cut the corners off all three pieces with a handsaw (Figure 4).

5. In the center of one octagon, drill an ⅛" diameter pilot hole and put it aside to use as the cover piece. Drill a ⅜" diameter hole in the center of a second octagon, then using a compass, draw in a 4" diameter circle centered in the third octagonal piece. Drill a ⅜" diameter hole on the inside edge of this circle to get the jigsaw blade in and saw out the circle (Figure 5).

6. Make another octagon from 7½" long one-by-eight cedar also with a 4" diameter hole in the center as described in Step 5. Glue and clamp the two octagons together with the 4" diameter holes perfectly lined up and the eight sides exactly parallel to each other (Figure 6). Plane a ¼" chamfer on each of the eight sides of the larger octagon (Figure 7). This will be the upper face with the smaller octagon on the underside.

7. Keeping the large octagon upside down, glue and nail (using galvanized finishing nails) each of the eight 12¾" cedar strips (Step 2) in the middle of each side of the two smaller octagons (Figure 8). Be careful to keep them perpendicular to the surface of the octagon. Now, before the glue dries, set this assembly right side up on a work surface and put finishing nails down through the chamfered octagon into the top of each cedar strip to pull them up tight to the top (Figure 9).

8. With the post embedded in the ground and the electrical wires protruding from the top, center the second octagon (with the ⅜" diameter hole in the center) over it, keeping the widest arms of the cruciform flush with two of the sides (Figure 10). Drill four ¼" pilot holes through the octagon into the ends (arms) of the post then fasten it down securely with four 2½" heavy duty roundhead brass or bronze

screws. Do not glue the octagon to the post to ensure that the finished lantern can be removed if necessary.

9. Screw an all-weather light socket (wired) to the center of the octagon.

10. Using glue and finishing nails, carefully nail the eight cedar strips to the middle of each side of the octagonal base. As shown in the side view, let the cedar strips hang down 2" below the bottom of the base. The lantern will be left with a large hole at the top to allow access to the light bulb and socket.

11. Use the first octagon, which was put aside, as a cover piece over the large access hole at the top of the lantern. Chamfer the edges and drill small pilot holes about ¹/₂" deep, about ⁵/₈" in from each of four opposite sides, on the underside of the cap. Hammer four common nails into these holes then trim the heads off with wire cutters, leaving 1¹/₄" of nail protruding (Figure 11). These nails will become "legs" to keep the cap approximately ³/₄" above the top of the lantern.

12. Carefully center the cover piece over the top of the lantern with sides parallel to each other. Press the cover piece down just hard enough for the nail to make an indent in the wood on the top of the lantern. Use these marks from the four nails as guides for drilling ¹/₂" deep holes slightly larger than the diameter of the nails. These holes will allow the nails to lift out of the holes easily after the cap is set in place.

13. Finally, glue and screw a 1¹/₂" cube of cedar (from the underside of the cover piece) in place to form a finishing detail on the top.

14. Finish the lantern with one of the many clear or tinted exterior finishes available at most paint or hardware stores or let it weather naturally. To increase the reflectivity of the lamp, paint the inside faces with white enamel before assembling. To reduce harsh light from the light bulb, place a cylinder of frosted Lexan® inside the lantern by tightly rolling a 9¹/₄" × 20" sheet (9¹/₄" long) and pushing it down through the large hole at the top. The stiffness of the sheet will allow it to spring out to form a cylinder.

NAIL

Figure 8

Figure 9

Figure 10

Figure 11

Fern (Shida) Post Lantern

The Fern is another version of a post lantern. It is more complex in appearance than the Iris, but the construction principles are the same. The flat sides on the Iris lantern obscure the light except at the corners. The Fern post lantern allows the light to emerge from within a circle of fins.

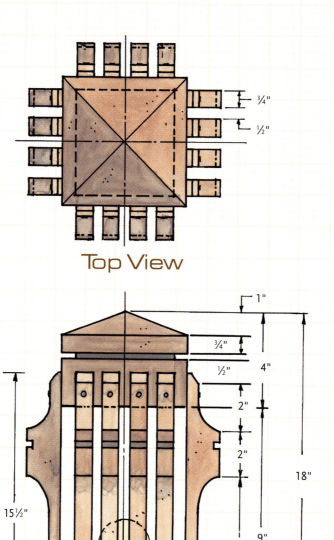

Top View

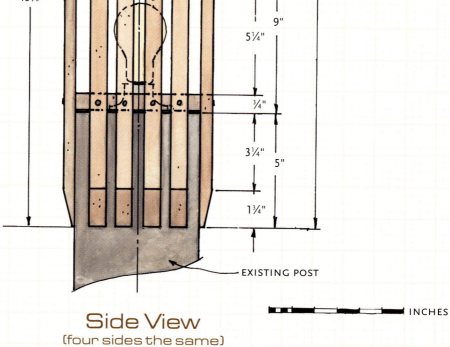

¾"
½"
1"
¾"
4"
½"
2"
2"
18"
9"
5¼"
¾"
3¼"
5"
1¾"
15½"

EXISTING POST

INCHES

Side View
(four sides the same)

Method

1. Using the top of an existing post as a pattern, shape the top of the lantern from a 4" long piece of cedar, 5$\frac{1}{2}$" square.

2. Plane four 1" deep bevels by drawing corner to corner diagonals.

3. To add an interesting detail to the top block, cut a $\frac{1}{4}$" × $\frac{1}{2}$" deep slot around it, 2" up from the bottom using a handsaw (see side view).

4. Cut a 3" diameter hole in the center of a $\frac{3}{4}$" × 5$\frac{1}{2}$" × 5$\frac{1}{2}$" red cedar bottom block, also shaped to match the top of the post (Figure 1).

5. By enlarging the side view on a photocopier, make a pattern of the shape of each of the sixteen fins (four on each side) from $\frac{3}{4}$" × 1$\frac{1}{2}$" × 16" cedar pieces using a jigsaw.

6. Nail the fins to the top with a 1$\frac{1}{2}$" overlap as shown and then nail them to the bottom piece. The bottom piece should be 5" from the ends of the fins (see dimensions on side view).

7. The finished lantern should fit snugly over the post without needing any extra fasteners.

To reduce the harshness of the light from the bulb, place a cylinder of frosted Lexan® inside the lantern. Roll an 8" × 18" sheet and push it up inside the lantern, letting it expand into a cylinder. Be sure to allow at least $\frac{1}{4}$" space above the Lexan® to avoid heat build-up.

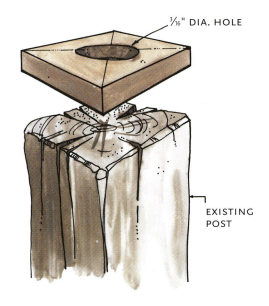

$\frac{3}{16}$" DIA. HOLE

EXISTING POST

Figure 1

Tools

- Tablesaw, handsaw, and jigsaw
- Drill with $\frac{1}{8}$" and $\frac{3}{8}$" diameter bits
- Hammer
- Bar-clamps – minimum two
- Heavy duty scissors
- Pair of wire cutters

Materials

- Top – red cedar block 4" long 5$\frac{1}{2}$" square cut from a six-by-six
- Bottom – $\frac{3}{4}$" thick red cedar, 5$\frac{1}{2}$" square
- Sides – sixteen fins cut from one-by-two red cedar, each 15$\frac{1}{2}$" long
- Frosted Lexan® sheet – 8" 18", available at plastic supply stores
- Nails – thirty-two 1$\frac{1}{4}$" long galvanized finishing nails
- Weatherproof electrical fixture and underground wiring

Hokkaido Outdoor Garden Lantern

This lantern is ideal for a garden path, either side of a driveway, or at the entrance to a house. It will require an underground, weather-proofed electrical wiring source with a remote switch. The project is intended to be mounted on a stone wall, but it could easily be worked into a rock garden or patio. The lantern itself is made of four glass panels in a heavy wood frame. The roof is made from a slab of sandstone, the weight of which holds the lantern in place. The stone slab should be light enough that it can easily be lifted off to provide access to the light fixture. A slab of concrete can also serve the same purpose. The rustic sophistication of this lantern adds charm and character to any landscaped area.

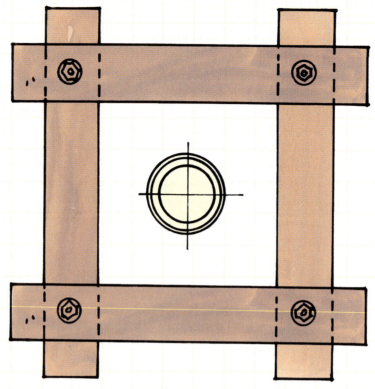

Top View

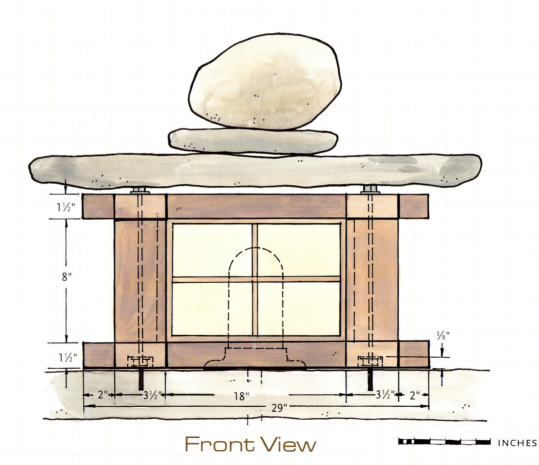

1½"

8"

1½"

⁵⁄₈"

2"   3½"   18"   3½"   2"

29"

Front View

INCHES

Method

1. Choose a slab of sandstone or concrete on which the lantern will rest. Drill a 2" diameter hole through the center of the slab with a masonry bit. There are a variety of weatherproof electrical socket fittings available that can be attached directly to the metal wiring conduit. This conduit must protrude from the top of the hole in the slab just enough to allow this.

2. Cut four pieces from four-by-four stock, 8" long.

3. Draw corner-to-corner diagonals on each end of each of the four corner pieces to locate the centers. With a $^5/_8$" diameter bit, drill through the center of each piece from each end, so the holes meet in the middle.

4. At one corner only of the long side of each piece cut a $^5/_8$" × $^5/_8$" rabbet on a tablesaw (Figure 1).

5. Using two-by-four stock, cut four pieces 23" long and four pieces 29" long. Cut a $^3/_4$" × $3^1/_2$" dado across each piece with a handsaw or tablesaw, 2" from each end, as shown in Figure 2. Assemble these pieces with lap joints as shown, to form the top and the bottom of the lantern.

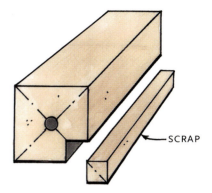

SCRAP

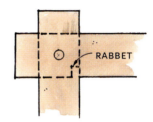

RABBET

Figure 1

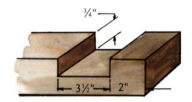

$^3/_4$"

$3^1/_2$"   2"

Figure 2

Tools
- Tablesaw and small crosscut handsaw
- Drill with $^1/_2$" and $^1/_4$" diameter wood bit as well as a $^1/_4$" diameter masonry bit
- Chisel – $^1/_2$" wide
- Adjustable wrench

Materials
- Corner posts – four wooden posts, $3^1/_2$" square × 8" long each
- Top and bottom crosspieces – eight, four: $1^1/_2$" × $3^1/_2$" × 23" each, four: $1^1/_2$" × $3^1/_2$" × 29" each
- Window glass – two panes: 8" × 13", and two panes: 8" × 19"
- Wood trim – twenty-four pieces each $^1/_4$" square × 12" long
- Glazier's points – two dozen (minimum)

- Brads – minimum four dozen $^5/_8$"
- Top slabs – one 1" thick sandstone (or concrete) slab 2" square, and one $1^1/_2$" thick sandstone (or concrete) slab 36" square
- Several interesting rocks for top of slabs
- Weatherproof electrical light fixture

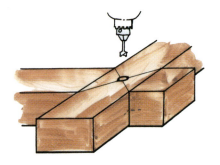

Figure 3

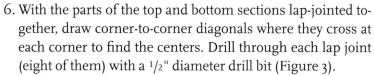

6. With the parts of the top and bottom sections lap-jointed together, draw corner-to-corner diagonals where they cross at each corner to find the centers. Drill through each lap joint (eight of them) with a $1/2$" diameter drill bit (Figure 3).

7. Bolt the entire assembly together using four $1/2$" diameter lag bolts (12" long) as shown in scale drawing. Use two washers with each bolt, one at the top so the head won't sink into the wood. The stone roof will rest on these bolts and provide a gap at the top of the lantern to allow heat from the bulb to escape. The bottom of the lantern should sit flat on the slab it rests upon; countersink the nut and washer at the end of each bolt. Do this before the $1/2$" diameter hole is drilled. Use a drill bit at least the same diameter as the washer and drill the hole about $5/8$" deep to completely bury the nut (Figure 4).

Figure 4

8. The bolts should now extend below the lantern. Center the lantern on its base (over the light bulb) and mark the position of each bolt. With a $5/8$" diameter masonry bit, drill four $1 1/2$" deep holes in the sandstone base to receive the bolt-ends of the lantern. These will keep the lantern from shifting on its base (Figure 5).

Figure 5

9. Place two 8" × 13" panes and two 8" × 19" panes of window glass inside the lantern frame as shown in Figure 6. Hold these panes in place with glazier's points top and bottom.

10. Apply the 1/4" square wood trim to the outside of the glass. This trim is decorative only; the glazier's points alone will hold the glass in place from the inside. Attach the trim around the edge of the opening with 5/8" brads (Figure 7). Joint the two center pieces into the perimeter trim as shown in Figure 8, lap-jointed at the center (Figure 9), and glued to the glass with construction cement.

11. Finish the lamp with linseed oil or any one of the wide variety of clear or tinted exterior finishes available from most hardware stores. Select several interesting rocks or stones to finish off the top of this lantern.

12. Rest the lantern frame on a large slab of sandstone or concrete. Drill a 2" diameter hole through the center of the slab with a masonry bit. There are a variety of weatherproof electrical socket fittings available that can be attached directly to the metal wiring conduit. This conduit must protrude from the top of the hole in the slab just enough to allow this.

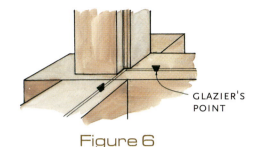

GLAZIER'S POINT

Figure 6

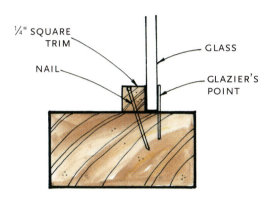

1/4" SQUARE TRIM

GLASS

NAIL

GLAZIER'S POINT

Figure 7

Figure 8

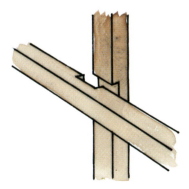

Figure 9

WIRING: SOCKET, SWITCH, AND PLUG

BRASS SLEEVE

CARDBOARD
SLEEVE

SOCKET
IN PLASTIC
"BODY"

KNOT

BRASS CUP

⅜" DIA.
BRASS NIPPLE

Figure 1

Most of the lamps in this book require only a socket (single or double), a length of two-strand lamp cord (electrical wire), a switch (on either the cord or in the socket), and a plug. All of these items can be purchased from a hardware or building supply store.

A standard brass socket is made up of four parts (Figure 1): the brass socket cap or base, the socket (with a switch built into the plastic "body" where the electrical wires are attached, or on the cord), a cardboard insulating sleeve, and the brass outer shell (which press-fits onto the base) holding the four pieces together as a single unit. The built-in switch can be either a push-button or a pull-chain. A switch located on a single bulb socket is impractical for some of the projects in this book. In these cases, buy a switch which can be mounted on a cord. The wall-light projects can be operated using the house electrical switches and circuits.

Electrical Sockets

The standard single bulb socket is secured to a lamp by means of a "nipple." This is a metal tube with threads on the outside, available in lengths from 1" to 12". The nipple is threaded part way into the lamp, and the lamp cord is pulled up through the lamp, through the nipple, and through the socket base. The base is threaded onto the nipple and held in place with a built-in set-screw. Separate the two wires of the lamp cord for 3" and then tie an "underwriter's knot" (reef knot) in it (as shown in Figure 2) to prevent the cord from being pulled out from the socket. Strip the plastic insulation from the ends of both wires for $3/8$" and twist the fine strands of each and shape the end of each wire into a hook, then attach to the socket's body with the screws provided. Assemble the socket, press-fitting the outer shell into the base. Note: DO NOT omit the cardboard insulating sleeve.

Figure 2

Double sockets (end to end on a single body) are readily available in ceramic without a switch and can be mounted on a nipple attached to a junction box cover (Figure 3). Note that this type of fixture has two threaded nipples attached, either one of which is used to secure the socket to a lamp and/or a wall-mounting bracket.

A switch of the type shown can be attached to the lamp cord itself. This type is readily available and comes with a set of instructions for how to attach it.

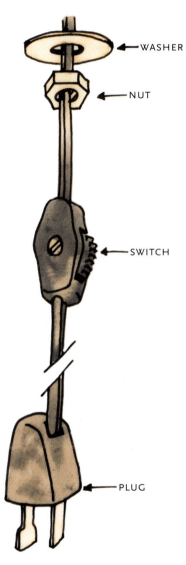

WASHER

NUT

SWITCH

PLUG

Figure 4

Figure 3

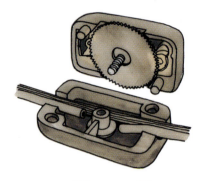

Figure 5

Attaching a Switch to a Cord

Make sure the cord is not plugged in and unscrew the switch cover. Carefully separate the two wires in the lamp cord for approximately 1". The plastic coating on most lamp cords is smooth over the one wire and ribbed over the other. In the middle of the separated area of the smooth wire only, cut a 1/4" gap.

Slip the cord inside the cover of the switch. The ridged wire should run through the open channel on one side of the center post and the ends of the smooth wire should lie in the divided channel on the other side of the post (Figure 5). Make sure that the ends do not touch or overlap the divider.

Fit the two halves of the switch together and put in the fastening screw. Squeeze the sections closed, forcing the metal teeth through the insulation of the hot wire. Finally, secure the screw with the small fastening provided.

Attaching a Plug

Finally, attach a plug at the end of the lamp cord, if it does not already have one. Two types of plugs are readily available: the polarized plug and the quick-connect plug. To attach the lamp cord to the polarized plug (Figure 6):

Push the lamp cord through the hole in the cover and split the wires 3" from the end of the cord. Strip 1/2" insulation from each wire.

Remove the cover of the new plug and loosen its terminal screws.

At the stripped end, twist the strands together, then loop them clockwise around the silver terminal. Tuck loose strands under the terminal before tightening the screws.

Fasten the smooth wires by twisting them together and then looping them clockwise around the brass terminal.

Finally, put the plug cover back on and then plug the lamp in.

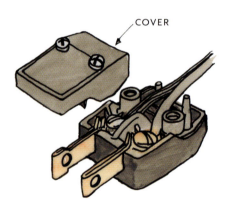

COVER

Figure 6

To attach a quick-connect plug to a lamp cord (Figure 7):

Cut the cord but don't strip the wire or allow any strands to protrude. Trim it if necessary to get a clean cut.

Press the blades of the plug together and pull the blade holder out of the casing.

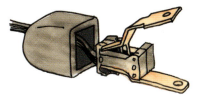

Figure 7

Thread the lamp cord through the back of the casing and spread the blades apart. Push the cord as far as possible into the holder, angling the lamp cord so that the ridged wire aligns with the tooth in the wide blade and the smooth wire aligns with the tooth of the narrow blade.

Push the blades together, forcing the tooth on each through the cord insulation. Slip the blade holder back into the casing and plug in the lamp.

SOURCES

Shoji (paper)

Practically speaking, any paper product that will shrink taut after being glued to a wooden frame can be used as shoji. For lamps and lanterns the paper should be thin enough to allow some degree of light through. Most very thin and translucent paper (known generically as "rice paper") is actually mulberry paper and is available in a variety of tones and textures from most paper supply or art supply stores. Paper suppliers may be found on the internet by searching Google® for *shoji paper.*

Plasticized Shoji

Plastic coated paper or simulated paper plastic sheet has the advantage of being rigid enough to stand on its own without having to be stretched. It will withstand heat better than regular paper and is available at cane or bamboo supply stores. Similar products are available by searching the internet for *fire resistant shoji paper.*

Lexan® or Acrylic Sheet

Heavy plastic sheets that can still be bent in a curve are available at most plastics supply stores. Or use *lexan* in your search engine.

Wood

The woods suggested in this book are readily available at lumberyards (softwood) and/or hardwood dealers.

Hardware

All hardware including lamp fittings and cords referred to in this book are available at most hardware stores.

Acknowledgements

I want to thank the whole staff at Hartley & Marks who experienced the vagaries of the production of this book as much as I did. I especially want to thank Vic Marks, who proposed the idea, for his support, advice, and patience through the process. I also want to thank managing editor, Susan Juby, for her advice, patience, and expert editorial help. Thanks also to computer-wizards John McKercher and Adina Crângea Costiuc for making my work presentable on the pages. My thanks and appreciation go out to Scott Banta who, following the first draft of the instructions, built some of these projects and made important corrections along the way. Without the ready assistance and enthusiasm of all of these people who kept the torches lit, this project might have stumbled in the dark.